RaugustReports

presents

15 Licensing Super Trends for 2015 and Beyond

RaugustReports

presents

15 Licensing Super Trends for 2015 and Beyond

by Karen Raugust

R A U G U S T

C O M M U N I C A T I O N S

Introduction

The business of licensed products and services has been reshaped in a number of significant ways over the past five to 10 years. Its transformation not only continues, but at a faster pace than ever before.

Licensors, licensees, agents, and retailers are dealing with new technologies that continually come on the scene. They are experimenting with novel business models. And they are trying to find untapped niches—whether property types, products, distribution channels, or geographic regions—to drive incremental royalty streams. New opportunities come and go with accelerated velocity.

In the context of this ever-evolving landscape, how can members of the licensing community position themselves for continued success?

Even as the nature of the licensing business seems to change daily, there are overriding trends that are likely to remain steady over the coming years and can help guide licensing executives as they face the future. This report outlines 15 of those overriding and often interrelated "licensing super trends." Each has an impact across property types, product categories, territories, and retail channels, and each is likely to last for the foreseeable future, providing a context for deal-making going forward.

Each chapter in this report focuses on one of the 15 overriding trends, including a discussion of some of the current shorter-term growth areas that illustrate the point. A variety of exhibits and mini-profiles adds further insight. At the end of the report, we identify the factors that tie together all 15 of the overriding trends, and take a look ahead. Collectively, the information contained herein provides a snapshot of the status of the licensing business in early 2015 and a glimpse into its future.

While most of the 15 trends discussed here provide licensors, licensees, and others involved in licensing with opportunities to enhance their businesses, much of the growth will be incremental. The licensing business remains competitive and difficult. In fact, it is the challenges inherent in today's licensing landscape that have given birth to most of these super trends and are propelling them forward.

1

Technology: The Only Constant Is Change

The ever-advancing technology landscape has fundamentally changed licensing in many ways, and will continue to do so. This evolution (or, in some cases, revolution) has ramifications on every facet of licensing: on the properties that are available, on new and existing product categories, on retailing, and on the way the licensing community does business.

With the increasingly fast pace of technological change, it is difficult to predict what specific technologies will take off in any given year. Some of the top trends in 2014—wearable technology, 3D printing, online-only distribution of entertainment vehicles, and the like—were barely on the radar in 2013.

So while the developments discussed in this section represent just a snapshot of a moment in time, the overarching trend of constant, quick, and sometimes fundamental technological progress will hold true going forward. The licensing community will continue to need to monitor all of these changes, not only to decide whether to jump in but also the right time to enter—and exit.

Rise of Wearable Technology

Wearable technology—which combines fashion and tech-driven functionality—came into its own as a viable licensing category in 2014. It continues to evolve quickly as new types of devices are introduced.

Most of the early activity centered on fitness wearables, such as activity trackers that allow users to measure their movement and other devices that monitor information such as calorie intake or vital signs.

Fitness, technology, and fashion brands (Skechers, Swarovski, Tory Burch, The Biggest Loser) all have entered the category through licensing, with the number of deals proliferating. Meanwhile, brands such as Weight Watchers and AccuWeather have licensed content for such devices.

Fitness Trackers for Total Fitness

Not surprisingly, athletic and fitness brands are among the properties active in lending their names to the wearable fitness tracker category. A case in point: FAM Brands' Bally Total Fitness, which has been licensed to Sakar International for fitness monitoring and related wearable devices. The initial line, introduced in 2015, includes dedicated activity trackers, activity-tracking watches, and heart rate monitors.

As of early 2015, wearables are quickly expanding beyond fitness trackers, with licensing potential growing along with the category. Examples include:

- Google Glass and similar eyewear. Diane von Furstenberg was one of the first licensors to enter this space, with her versions of Google Glass selling through Net-a-Porter. Musician/entrepreneur will.i.am is developing his own smartglasses, as are Intel and Luxottica, the latter the eyewear licensee for a raft of fashion labels.

- Smartbands and smartwatches. Guess? is among the properties that have lent their names to smartwatches, while Intel partnered with fashion retailer Opening Ceremony to design its MICA smartband. (Smartbands are like fitness trackers, but provide information beyond just fitness.) With Apple set to enter the smartwatch segment in 2015, most observers are bullish about the growth prospects for these devices.

- Technology-embedded apparel and accessories. Fabrics with integrated sensors can monitor temperature, heart rate, and communications, protect against microbes or theft, or serve other functions. Ralph Lauren introduced a biometric shirt in partnership with tech firm OMsignal at the 2014 U.S. Open, with plans for retail distribution in 2015; Intel teamed with designer Anouk Wipprecht to design a smart dress; and Macy's launched leather accessories from designer Andrew Royce Bauer that incorporate anti-theft technology.

- Smartphones. Falling into the wearables segment thanks to their ubiquity in daily life, smartphones have recently emerged as potential licensed products. Many of the properties involved to date, which range from Caterpillar to Nokia, are tech brands, but some lend specific attributes (such as ruggedness in the case of Caterpillar).

- Mobile payment devices. With entrepreneurs and established business people taking their sales operations on the road, some want to add a fashion flair to devices such as the Square. Designer Vivienne Tam was one of the first to enter this segment.

- Clip-ons. Companies are introducing devices that clip to a purse or clothing and perform many of the same tasks as a smartband or smartwatch. BeBop and Simple Matters are among the companies marketing various types of wearable sensors.

Established product categories such as headphones, earbuds, and electronics accessories also are a form of wearable technology, of course, and they have been and remain active for licensing.

It is hard to say at this point which of the items listed above, or other wearable technologies, will take hold and which will fail or be short-term novelties. But licensors and licensees will continue to experiment with how to make the marriage between technology and fashion, pop culture, and other properties work.

Toy Tech With A Reason for Being

Many pairings of licensing and technology start out as novelties, allowing the licensor and licensee to stand out from their competition but not generating significant revenues or establishing a long-term business. More and more, however, these types of initiatives quickly evolve into viable business models with a real purpose and the involvement of many properties and products.

A good example is the toy industry. As recently as early 2012, toy companies starting touting the fact that they had included an app with their physical toys to add a dimension of "augmented reality" (AR). Typically the apps scanned the product and provided some sort of little extra, like an animation or a 3D representation of an image. The feature typically added a novelty twist to the product, but was not integral to its enjoyment.

Similar augmented-reality initiatives soon started to expand into other product categories, as well, from food packaging to t-shirts to children's books to bed throws.

The connection between physical and digital has evolved at a fast pace, however, especially in the toy space. A large percentage of physical toys continue to include apps, but they more frequently provide a real enhancement to game play. For example, rather than simply adding an animation clip, an app may unlock some facts that are critical to game play; offer play value in the form of additional games, storylines, or character bios; or be used to operate the physical toy (such as using an app to fly a toy airplane, in lieu of traditional remote-control technologies).

Meanwhile, technology integration has moved beyond apps to products where digital and physical components are of equal importance. A key illustration is the growth of digital-plus-physical toys along the lines of Activision's Skylanders, which pioneered this space, and Disney Infinity, which appeared soon thereafter.

Other examples include:
- DreamWorks and Fuhu's partnership to pair the former's How to Train Your Dragon with the latter's Morpho Pods.

- Hasbro and Rovio's alliance to combine the former's Telepods into a new iteration of the latter's flagship brand, with Angry Birds GO!

- Lego's Fusion line, where an app allows mobile devices to identify the bricks used to build something on its surface, then imports the creation into a mobile game using the camera function.

- Nintendo's amiibo, which pairs physical and digital play based on Nintendo's internally developed properties (e.g. Super Mario Bros.) and a few outsiders (Pokémon).

Advancements in AR have extended to other products as well. The Tamagotchi Friends fashion line from Evy of California, through a deal between licensor Bandai America and Sync Beatz Entertainment, allows girls to use their devices to scan a marker on the fabric, customize selfies with Tamagotchi elements, and put the photos on digital ID cards that are shareable on social media.

Similar evolutions of technology are happening quickly in other categories as well.

Traditional Categories Transformed

While emerging technologies create opportunities for brand-new licensing arenas, possibly the more profound impacts are on existing categories where technology has disrupted or is in the midst of disrupting traditional business models. Much of the attention has been on such transformations in the distribution of content, as in the music, movie, and book industries.

But technological evolutions and revolutions have affected traditional physical product categories as well. Email has replaced sales of stationery, invitations, and greeting cards, for example, leading that business to go digital.

Designers such as Kate Spade, Charlotte Ronson, Oscar de la Renta, Georgina Chapman, and others, along with characters such as SpongeBob and celebrities such as Victoria Justice, have met this challenge by creating collections of digital and print-on-demand stationery for companies such as Tiny Prints, Paperless Post, and One Kings Lane.

Artists, too, have gone digital in this category, as with Bonnie Marcus's deal with

Kodak Alaris for print-on-demand cards available through kiosks in CVS and Target stores. Many of the deals include both printed and digital products, while others focus on digital only.

Potentially transformational technologies on the horizon could affect other industries as well. Virtual reality (as exemplified by the VR technology from Oculus Rift) generated buzz in 2014 and could ultimately have a strong impact on interactive gaming and potentially on entertainment viewing. The technology puts the user into a virtual 3D world through the use of a VR headset.

One licensor experimenting with VR technology is Hasbro, which partnered with Google's Project Tango in mid-2014 to create a Transformers tablet with a special camera that allows the user to experience a giant virtual Optimus Prime. Several entertainment and gaming studios are developing content for the technology.

Another type of virtual reality that is growing, although it may not have as great an impact as Oculus Rift or Project Tango-style innovations, is the development of virtual "holographic" characters that can appear in live theatrical productions, as well as in traditional and digital media. Authentic Brands Group has granted Pulse Evolution the rights to develop virtual performance opportunities for Elvis Presley and Marilyn Monroe.

It should be noted that some categories expected to feel negative ramifications from new technologies are still going strong. Observers predicted that traditional watches would decline as a category for licensing since many consumers check the time on their phones and do not wear wristwatches. But traditional watches remain a very active category as fashion accessories, with labels such as Reebok and Coach extending and expanding their watch collections and the likes of Filson and Tory Burch entering the category for the first time.

Emergence of 3D Printing

Many experts believe it will be five years to a decade (if ever) before 3D printing becomes widely used by mainstream consumers. Still, 2014 was a watershed year for this technology in terms of the number of licensors that began experimenting with it.

Property owners' objectives typically do not center on significant revenue-generation at this point; rather, the goal is to offer fans a new means of engagement by generating their own personalized content in 3D form (within limits). In addition, the licensors want to position themselves for the future in case the technology does take off.

Many of the licensing-related ventures in 3D printing to date have been in the entertainment/character arena, with examples including CBS Consumer Products (Star Trek), Disney/Marvel, Hasbro, Uglydoll, Sesame Workshop, and Warner Bros. (The Hobbit).

3D Printing: A Good Thing

A deal in late 2014 between Martha Stewart Living Omnimedia and MakerBot was significant in that it encompassed both patterns and filament, while most licenses involving 3D printing so far have focused on a limited range of patterns only. The initial three uniquely colored filaments—the filament is the material (a plastic in this case) that the printer uses to create the products—represent MakerBot's first co-branded collection.

In addition, the deal's focus is on items for daily use, as opposed to the novelties and collectibles that are the bread and butter of licensed 3D-printed products to date. The initial Martha Stewart patterns, dubbed the Trellis Collection, include designs for coasters, napkin rings, votive holders, place card holders, and other table accessories. Designs cost $.99 each, or $2.99 for the entire collection.

Consumers who do not own a 3D printer can purchase and print the products in MakerBot stores.

Licensors of interactive gaming properties, such as Ubisoft for Assassin's Creed, Mojang for Minecraft, Harmonix for Rock Band, and Blizzard for World of Warcraft, also have a strong early presence. And other property types, such as sports, fashion designers, musicians, and others, also are experimenting with the technology.

Most of the ventures have centered on unique collectibles, but more licensors ahead are likely to focus on personalization of mainstream items such as fashion accessories (e.g. selecting a custom buckle for a purse) or tableware (choosing from a variety of designs and colors to create a custom piece).

Even 3D printing hardware has seen some licensing activity. Ekocycle, the partnership between Coca-Cola and will.i.am, licensed 3D Systems for a consumer printer using filament made partly from plastic Coke bottles. Hershey is working with 3D Systems to develop a chocolate printer.

The 3D printing landscape is fragmented so far, with many potential technology partners and fan communities available to work with licensors. Some that have partnered with IP owners, or have announced their intention to do so, include 3D Systems/Cubify, Stratasys/MakerBot, 3 DLT, and Shapeways. However, many other companies, from Staramba to 3DPlusMe to ZCorp, have participated in selected ventures, and more potential partners are coming on the scene almost every day.

It should be noted that in addition to sanctioned ventures in conjunction with property owners, the world of 3D printing also includes a lot of true user-generated content, with fans printing unique LEGO pieces they need for a building project, or creating weapons or costume components tied to a game, TV show, or comic book.

This brings up a key challenge for licensors: namely, the ramifications of 3D printing on intellectual property protection. At some point in the future, many experts believe, consumers will easily be able to create their own designs (sometimes integrating licensed properties) and sell them. They will even be able to scan licensed products and replicate them through 3D printing. Some companies are likely to sell counterfeit 3D printing blueprints using licensors' IPs.

While most such uses are clearly unlawful, it will be difficult for licensors to police the market when manufacturing is in the hands of individuals rather than in the more concentrated hands of a relatively few manufacturers. The same is true for any kind of user-generated content, but the commercial potential of 3D printed items may exceed that associated with most fan-generated artwork.

The day when mainstream consumers are competing with licensors and licensees may be far off, however. The 3D printing industry must pass a number of milestones before the technology becomes widespread. Some key criteria include:

- A wider selection of better-quality and easier-to-use printers available, at a range of price points.

- Wider distribution of printers and scanners.

- More blueprints available to make it easy for customers to design and print objects.

- The resolution of IP issues so consumers can select from a range of officially licensed items to print legally.

- More service providers in place to assist consumers in designing and printing objects or do it for them.

- More opportunities for consumers to try 3D printing or see it in action, whether at retail or events.

The year 2014 brought significant movement along many of these measurements. Mass retailers began supporting 3D printing, for example, with Home Depot selling hardware and the UPS Store and Staples among those providing 3D printing services. Meanwhile, small specialty stores focusing on 3D printing are expanding beyond the biggest cities into malls across the country.

More consumers also are being exposed to the technology at concerts, sports events, and comic conventions; communities and services such as Shapeways are gaining traction with early adopters; and more marketers are offering limited amounts of customization through 3D printing.

A case in point: Target partnered with Shapeways for a 2014 holiday collection of customizable jewelry and ornaments, with consumers able to choose their own combinations of size, color, materials (from plastic to metal), and inscriptions.

Finally, new and improved printers are being introduced (or their development crowdfunded) almost daily.

Licensors are, therefore, increasingly dipping their toes into the 3D printing waters.

Some offer very little customization, while others are letting consumers drive the boat to a much higher degree. But their interest in the technology should continue as they try to position themselves for success when the 3D printing industry matures and the technology's mainstream uses become clearer.

Exhibit 1

Selected Digital-Origin Properties Available for Licensing, by Source

Property Source	Types of Properties in Sector	Selected Examples of Properties	Typical Licensing Activity
YouTube (DIY)	Cat videos, "let's play" videos, DIY musicians and entertainers, home-based cooking shows, fan-generated/indie animation.	Grumpy Cat, Justin Bieber, Mr. Stampy, Annoying Orange, L'il Bub, What Does the Fox Say?, Dumb Ways to Die, Sophia Grace and Rosie, Kid President, ItsJudysLife, PewDiePie, SMOSH, Cimorelli, Mashimaro.	Largely collectibles and content-based items. Examples: Mr. Stampy t-shirts from Spreadshirt, Li'l Bub plush from Cuddle Barn, Grumpy Cat puzzles from TCG, What Does the Fox Say? children's books from Simon & Schuster.
Blogs/Bloggers	Fashion and style blogs, mommy blogs, food and cooking blogs, home and lifestyle blogs.	Aimee Song/Song of Style, Leandra Medine/Man Repeller, Apartment Therapy, Michelle Phan, Mrs. Lilien, Bryan Grey Yambao/Bryanboy, Cupcakes and Cashmere, Tina Craig and Kelly Cook/Bag Snob, Bakerella, Gabi Gregg/GabiFresh, Theo & Beau/Momma's Gone City.	Categories closely related to blog content, often in the form of limited collaborations. Examples: Man Repeller sneakers with Superga, Michelle Phan cosmetics with L'Oreal, Bryanboy furs with Adrienne Landau, Bag Snob handbags with Artisan House, GabiFresh swimsuits with SwimsuitsForAll.com
Other Social Media	Celebrities and brands made famous through Twitter, Pinterest, Vine, and Instagram, texting/chatting avatars, and other social media properties. Many also have blogs but their awareness is driven by these social media.	Rob Delaney, @IQuoteForHer, Bethany Mota, Joy Cho/Oh Joy, @Queen_UK, Jan Halvorson/Poppytalk, Jack and Jack, LINE Friends, Kate Arends/Wit & Delight, Nash Grier, Hayes Grier, Cameron Dallas, Carter Reynolds, Tuzki.	Either collectible (analogous to DIY YouTube strategies) or limited brand-extension (analogous to bloggers). Examples: Bethany Mota for apparel, accessories, and jewelry at Aeropostale; Rob Delaney board game; Poppytalk, Wit & Delight, and Oh Joy for limited stationery and decor collections at Target.
Gaming	Mobile gaming apps, virtual worlds, online MMOs.	Minecraft, Angry Birds, Moshi Monsters, Temple Run, Fruit Ninja, Flappy Bird.	Sometimes launched/pitched as wide, character-based consumer products programs but most are focused on physical games, gaming accessories, publishing, and some novelties (t-shirts, plush). A few, such as Angry Birds and Minecraft, break this mold and are widely licensed.
Online Networks/ Websites	Digital-only platforms, both independent and studio-run.	AwesomenessTV, BeFit, Funny or Die, Allrecipes.	Broader programs than most digital properties, either tied to content or celebrity-driven. Examples: BeFit-branded supplements with Top Secret Nutrition, AwesomenessTV apparel and accessories with Kohl's.

Note: Excludes professionally produced properties, from established entertainment studios, that are distributed digitally.
Source: Raugust Communications

Digital Platforms as a Source of Properties

It was just a couple of years ago that mobile apps and virtual worlds started to come on the scene as licenseable properties, following the success of Angry Birds from the mobile gaming arena and Moshi Monsters (especially in the U.K.) from the virtual world space.

Neither of these sectors has proven to be a consistent source of licensing hits; in fact, few properties beyond the pioneers have succeeded to any widespread degree. But Angry Birds, Moshi Monsters, and others paved the way for the wide variety of digital-origin properties that have proliferated and diversified in the short time since.

Exhibit 1 offers a snapshot of the types of digital properties available for licensing. They can be categorized into five major groups (excluding entertainment vehicles created by professionals and distributed via online platforms, discussed in Chapter 5):

- DIY productions distributed through YouTube.

- Blogs and bloggers.

- Properties from other social media platforms (e.g. Twitter, Pinterest, Instagram, texting/chatting services).

- Online- and mobile-origin gaming properties.

- Branded online networks, both independent and studio-run.

Each sector has been ongoing long enough that it has developed its own characteristics when it comes to licensing. Most of the programs remain niche in nature, with products primarily limited in availability or quantity (although some have broken out into longer-term deals). And categories tend to be very close to the property's core, although some have tried to extend beyond that and a few have succeeded in doing so.

Not surprisingly, the landscape for digital-origin properties is changing as fast as any sector in licensing. Bloggers came on the scene as licensable properties only in 2013, and as of early 2015 there are so many that they already fall into a number of sub-sectors, including fashion/beauty/style bloggers, foodies, home/lifestyle mavens, and mommy bloggers, among others.

Meanwhile, starting in 2014, the licensing community has begun to view other social media platforms—Pinterest, Instagram, Vine, instant messaging—as viable platforms to support licensing. Key retailers have created consumer products initiatives with celebrities from these platforms, including Target (with a group of three Pinners) and Aeropostale (first with Bethany Mota and then a group of four Vine celebs under the UNITED XXVI Collection banner).

Most celebrities and other properties that originate in the digital world—like properties of all kinds these days—rely on a multiplatform strategy to build awareness. While a particular property may be associated primarily with a blog or Pinterest, they typically are available to their fans through all social media venues.

One reason that digital-origin licensing has taken off so fast is that the sheer numbers of fans and followers associated with the top properties have spiked so quickly:
- As of mid-2014, fashion blogger Aimee Song, who has participated in collabo-

rations with the likes of Valentino and Saks Fifth Avenue, had more than 1.45 Instagram followers and 3.47 million page views on her blog, plus additional fans through Facebook, Twitter, and Pinterest.

- Bethany Mota, a fashion/style Instagrammer and vlogger whose apparel, accessories, and jewelry are sold at Aeropostale, has 2.5 million followers on Instagram, 5.6 million subscribers on YouTube, and 1.3 million followers on Twitter.

- The three Pinners with whom Target has teamed for party goods collections have millions of followers, including 13.6 million for Joy Cho, 8.3 million for Jan Halvarson, and 2.6 million for Kate Arends.

The sheer numbers, while impressive, do not tell the whole story of these properties' appeal. Many social media celebrities have significant roles as influencers, with their styles, purchasing habits, and lifestyle choices emulated by their fans. Thus the top properties have credibility in the consumer products space beyond the pure numbers.

That said, the nature of digital distribution means that fragmentation is a concern. Many properties from social media have intense groups of fans but are unknown by mainstream consumers, which may give some licensees and retailers pause. In addition, consumers' interests and purchase desires change quickly, especially in the social media space, meaning some of these properties are likely to have short lifespans in licensing.

However, given the more niche nature of licensing in general, these challenges are less and less of a barrier, especially given the strong numbers these properties can generate within their niche, not to mention the influence they can have on those fans.

Tech Drives Marketing and Distribution

Naturally, the fast-changing digital landscape is also having a significant impact on the marketing of licensed products. Licensing executives are struggling with how to best use social media, in all its various forms, to promote their products. Unlike traditional forms of media, where licensors and licensees are guided by a historical track record, much of the activity in digital channels is necessarily done on the fly.

Among the challenges associated with social media marketing:
- The fragmentation of the audience, making it difficult to select the right platform to reach fans.

- The difficulty of creating a marketing message that can break through, while not alienating consumers.

- The consumer-driven nature of social media, which creates a fine line between spurring viral word of mouth and losing control.

- The difficulty of creating a direct connection between a message and a purchase; this tie has been perceived as a benefit of online versus traditional marketing, but the extension to social media has proven challenging.

- The speed with which new social media platforms rise and fall, with Facebook's influence replaced by Pinterest and Instagram, then by Vine, then by whatever comes next.

- The multiple platforms (social media, websites) and devices (phones, tablets, laptops) on which consumers are social, requiring optimization of the message, visuals, and technology for all.

- The difficulty of building on success, since things change so fast.

Despite these barriers, marketing via social media is a necessity in today's world. Therefore licensors and licensees continue to experiment, and often succeed, as each new platform emerges:

- Vine has been a focus for marketing campaigns since late 2013, with properties including Uglydoll, Peanuts, Disney characters, and Blue Diamond (with its Almond Breeze milk alternative, manufactured under license by HP Hood) among those using the platform. The licensors of Paddington and Cut the Rope marketed their movie and mobile game, respectively, with a series of Vine influencer-produced videos distributed on Vine and Instragram.

- Mommy bloggers and YouTube-based child toy reviewers (EvanYouTubeHD, KittiesMama, etc.) have become important influencers when it comes to children's products.

- Social communities are key platforms for marketing, especially between key promotional or entertainment initiatives. Lionsgate partnered with Google's Art, Copy & Code project to market *The Hunger Games: Mockingjay Part I* to its fan communities through original indie-animator-created YouTube content.

Social platforms are taking off all across the world, in many cases (e.g. China and much of the rest of Asia) even more so than in North America. Brazilian football club CR Flamengo has used an online technology called WISfans to allow its current and former players to connect with fans across all social media and sports platforms, to name just one example of a global initiative.

This chapter has only touched on the ramifications of technology on the licensing business. Other areas that have been significantly affected range from the distribution of products and content to the importance of personalization and customization. These and other topics are addressed throughout this report.

2

Need for Speed

Technology has caused the pace of the licensing business to speed up, thanks to a number of factors on both the supply side and the demand side:

- The impact of social media, which assists properties in rising and falling faster and on a global basis, although frequently with a niche fan base.

- Changing entertainment distribution models, which have resulted in a transition from traditional television schedules to binge-watching.

- Improvements in manufacturing, which shorten the product-development process in many categories.

- The mainstreaming of print-on-demand technologies, which make it possible to produce and sell merchandise more quickly than the traditional process of manufacturing and shipping to retail.

- The emergence of "made in my own country" production as a viable strategy, due to lower cost structures, which reduces time to market.

Earlier Launches

Historically, a lag time of at least a year—especially in the entertainment sector—has been typical between the launch of a new property and the placement of licensed products at retail. Risk-averse licensors, licensees, and retailers wanted to ensure that there was adequate demand, and that the demand was likely to last a while, before they fully supported a licensing program.

While licensing executives remain as risk-averse as ever, they also realize that, if a property takes off, demand for products will hit immediately. Consumers want merchandise now, and they aren't willing to wait. Furthermore, with consumer tastes ebbing and flowing as quickly as they do these days, demand may have already waned by the time a full licensing program is developed and sold in to retail.

As a result, properties and their associated licensed products are coming to market faster than ever before:

- Merchandise tied to TV shows is starting to appear on store shelves less than a year after launch, not only for franchise-based properties such as Dora & Friends or WWE Slam City, but for brand-new properties such as Disney's Sofia the First or Nickelodeon's BLAZE. Retailer and licensee risk-averseness means this is possible only for properties backed by the biggest licensors, however.

- Licensing programs featuring emerging, relatively unknown designers, such as GQ and Gap's partnership for the magazine's menswear designers of the year, allow fans to purchase items soon after their discovery of a particular designer and before that designer hits it big. The program offers something fresh at retail, involves a group of designers rather than forcing the retailer to put all its eggs in one designer's basket, and may allow one or more of the young creators to break into the mainstream.

- Social media properties are able to get to retail quickly before demand wanes. When the Norwegian music-comedy video "What Does the Fox Say?" went viral globally in 2013, items such as t-shirts appeared at retailers including Target almost immediately, capitalizing on the property's short window at the peak of pop culture.

Of course, some product categories take longer to get to market than others. Soft goods such as t-shirts and other apparel items can arrive on store shelves very quickly these days, but other products, such as most toys or footwear, still require a longer timeframe for development, tooling, and manufacturing.

Print on Demand

It has become almost a prerequisite for properties of all types to make a limited range of products available on the key print-on-demand sites, such as CaféPress, Zazzle, or others. These platforms allow personalization—to various degrees depending on the licensor—but they also ensure that consumers can get their hands on products even while the property appeals only to a small core of consumers,

A Varied Print-on-Demand Landscape

Almost every licensed (or licensable) property these days has tie-in merchandise available through at least one print-on-demand platform. This includes the whole gamut of properties, from those that are heavily licensed into every category at retail to those with little to no bricks-and-mortar presence.

Marvel's 2014 tentpole film *Guardians of the Galaxy* is an example of the former. A month prior to the movie's release in theaters (and timed to the San Diego Comic-Con), CaféPress launched a wide line of t-shirts, hoodies, baseball jerseys, bags, smartphone cases, and other products, many with exclusive (including fan-generated) designs. The launch occurred shortly before the property's extensive range of traditional licensed products hit retail.

At about the same time and on the other end of the spectrum, the hamburger restaurant chain Red Robin launched a site on CaféPress to offer its customers a selection t-shirts, mugs, totes, aprons, clocks, and iPhone cases. Most featured the chain's advertising slogans or common social media phrases with a Red Robin twist. The chain has almost no retail presence with non-foods merchandise, although it has a licensing deal in place with ConAgra for seasoned steak fries sold in supermarkets.

or when mainstream demand hits quickly and products are not yet available in stores.

Niche properties rely on these sites as their primary retail channel, new properties use them to gauge and satisfy demand early in their lives, and global properties use them as a means of entering new markets. But even the biggest, most mainstream, most heavily licensed properties have a presence on print-on-demand platforms, both to give consumers personalization options and as a means of meeting demand prior to wide retail availability.

There are many print-on-demand options available to licensors, aside from the best-known venues for licensed products, such as CaféPress. Some property owners, such as the U.S. sports leagues, offer their own print-on-demand options; licensees in the stationery, wall décor, and other categories often can supply print-on-demand items; and there are many specialist print-on-demand e-tailers that focus on certain categories or property types. All enhance licensors' and licensees' ability to get products into consumers' hands quickly, among other benefits.

In and Out

The establishment of fast fashion and limited editions/capsule collections as a key strategy for certain retailers, and licensors, also is related to the need for speed when it comes to satisfying consumer demand.

As noted throughout this report, fast fashion strategies consisting of an ongoing program of short-term designer collaborations, as well as one-off collections that are limited in number of items, quantities, and/or time available, have a number of benefits for the partners. These range from providing something new to attract consumers again and again and cement their loyalty, to generating awareness and press coverage, to allowing a retailer or marketer a way to differentiate itself from its competition.

But they also fit with the fact that consumer tastes change quickly. Shoppers are excited about designers when they first appear in the store, as illustrated by Target's partnerships with Prabal Gurung, Jason Wu, and others, which sold out immediately. Once designer collections have been on shelf for a while, however, fans' attention tends to migrate in other directions. This is especially true as designers, celebrities, and other property types reach out to consumers via social media, making a closer connection and driving demand, but also playing into the tendency for consumers to be capricious, moving from one interest to another quickly.

As Exhibit 2 shows, players in fast fashion are predominantly global fashion specialty chains that have made this one of their key strategies, or mass, mid-tier, and some higher-end department store retailers who have incorporated this tactic as part of their positioning. The exhibit highlights retailers that either are U.S.-centric or operate across multiple territories, but some locally focused retailers also rely on fast fashion as a core component of their business. Lindex, a retailer that is strongest in the Nordic region, has collaborated with the likes of Jean-Paul Gaultier and Matthew Williamson, for example.

Some retailers are categorized as fast fashion because they change their merchandise mix frequently, but rarely do designer collaborations (e.g. Zara). Others that are not traditionally viewed as fast fashion chains sometimes will participate in fast fashion-like collaborations (e.g. J. Crew with Prabal Gurung). And the retailers that have long relied on a fast-fashion strategy often tweak or course-correct in terms of specific tactics, brand names, and the types of partners with which they associate.

It should be noted that characters also are the focus of collaborations with many of the retailers discussed here, in addition to the more common celebrity and designer deals. H&M, Uniqlo, Forever 21, and others have brought in a variety of entertainment properties and classic characters and given them a unique fashion flair through short-term collections.

The fast-fashion trend has been going strong since at least the mid-2000s. But more retailers continue to enter into collaborations (e.g. Lane Bryant and Dress Barn, both owned by Ascena, have been recent participants), whether through an ongoing strategy or a series of one-offs. More designers, especially on the luxury end, also continue to forge their first "fast-fashion" deals to get their products into the hands of more consumers and expand their mainstream awareness. Some, such as Jason Wu and Derek Lam, have made fast fashion a key component of their business over time and have partnered with several different retailers.

Exhibit 2

Selected U.S. and Global Players in Fast Fashion Retail

Retailer	Retail Channel	Selected Collaborations Over Time
Kohl's	Mid-tier	Milly by Michelle Smith, Peter Som, Elie Tahari, Derek Lam, Narciso Rodriguez. Fast fashion is under DesigNation label.
Target	Mass	Altuzarra, Philip Lim, Jason Wu, Proenza Schouler, Thakoon, Tara Jarmon, Peter Pilotto, Alexander McQueen, Rodarte, Missoni, Prabal Gurung. Has used various brand names over the years for its fast fashion programs.
Uniqlo	Specialty	Jil Sander, NIGO, Lulu Guinness, Costello Tagliapietra, Velvet, Karen Walker, many others; also partners with a variety of characters; some collaborations are global and some focused on certain regions. Some are co-branded with in-house labels such as Lifewear or UT.
Gap	Specialty	Diane von Furstenberg, GQ emerging menswear designers, Valentino, Alexander Wang.
Forever 21	Specialty	Petro Zilla, Rory Beca, Brian Lichtenberg, Disney.
Sears/Kmart	Mid-tier/Mass	Kelly Renee, JWK; also longer-term programs with Adam Levine, Nicki Minaj. Launched Now + Here fast fashion program in spring 2014.
Macy's	Department	Karl Lagerfeld, Made, Alberta Ferretti, Giambattista Valli, Francisco Costa, Nicole Richie. Also has long-term collaborations, as with Ryan Seacrest.
Topshop	Specialty	Meadham Kirchhoff, Heidi Klum, Christopher Kane, Mary Katrantzou, JW Anderson, Kate Moss; also longer-term collaborations, as with Beyoncé.
H&M	Specialty	Karl Lagerfeld, Lanvin, Stella McCartney, Comme des Garçons, Jimmy Choo, Roberto Cavalli, Versace, Victor & Rolf, Matthew Williamson, Marni, Maison Martin Margiela, Isabel Marant.

Source: Raugust Communications

The fortunes of fast-fashion retailers such as H&M and Uniqlo may rise and fall cyclically depending on economic and other trends, but the role of fast fashion within the licensing business is here to stay in the foreseeable future. With consumers always looking for something new and their tastes changing rapidly, an evolving landscape of designers within certain retail settings has become almost an expectation.

Property Lifespan Versus Product Development

The increasingly fast pace of the licensing business naturally raises a range of challenges. While manufacturing techniques have progressed and shortened lead times in many categories, the time needed for licensed products to go from deal signing to retail introduction remains slow compared to the speed at which properties can rise and fall in popularity.

Some of the key barriers to speedy development and delivery of merchandise include:
- Tooling and other time-consuming elements of the manufacturing process in hard goods categories.

- Complex product development processes that require time, such as in content-driven categories or sensory categories (e.g. fragrance).

- Intricate approval processes, which affect those categories with complex development processes but also are driven by licensor standards.

- Shipping from far-away manufacturing regions, such as China or other countries in Asia.

These factors have less of an impact on soft goods such as apparel or bedding than they do on categories such as toys, jewelry, footwear, publishing, and fragrance.

The increasingly speedy pace of licensing also runs counter to strategic considerations that licensors, and often their partners, put at a premium, notably the need to reduce risk and the desire to create a long-term business surrounding their property. Both have historically dictated a slow and steady build early in a property's life span.

The faster rise and fall of consumer demand these days, however, means that a property can hit quickly and strongly. For some—such as those targeting teens and propelled by social media—consumers may have moved on already by the time products hit the market.

The problem can also affect more traditional properties, which are concerned about not killing demand by saturating the market too early. While consumers may still want the property by the time products appear on store shelves, they may also be angry that merchandise is not available as soon as they want it. Such was the case with Disney's Frozen, which broke out fast in late 2013 and has remained hot through 2014 into 2015. Extreme shortages occurred in the first year of that time span and even beyond.

These types of timing issues have always been part of the nature of licensing, but the speed at which a property can gain and lose popularity is much more intense, meaning that providing the right quantities and mix of SKUs at the right time is arguably more difficult than ever.

Licensees are aware of the challenges and are streamlining their operations so they can better meet market demand. Concept One, an apparel and accessories licensee, has noted that it intends to continue to match its headwear, bags, and cold-weather apparel with pop culture brands, bringing products to market quickly "to maximize the trend opportunity." One of the licenses it signed in 2014 was the mobile game Flappy Bird.

3 Function First

Functional and performance characteristics have become key elements of many licensing deals and promise to become further entrenched. This trend takes many forms, from the addition of ingredients, technical performance, or other functional attributes, to the growth in rugged, work-ready merchandise, to the creation of licensed products of which the purpose is wholly utilitarian.

Functional and Performance Attributes

A functional or performance attribute in a licensed product line can emanate from the licensor's brand, as is the case with Church & Dwight's Arm & Hammer, which was a pioneer in this space. It has granted licensing rights for products ranging from bedding to pet dental care, each reflecting the brand's promise of cleanliness and, specifically, odor and stain control.

Celebrity + Performance = Competitive Advantage

A number of deals for performance apparel have centered on actresses and singers lending their names for lines of clothing that have technical attributes for working out, but also are fashionable enough to wear throughout a woman's busy day.

One recent example is singer Beyoncé's 50/50 joint venture with the British fast fashion retailer TopShop to create ParkwoodTop-Shop Athletic. The new company is producing an athletic streetwear collection to launch in fall 2015, with products extending across the dance, fitness, and sports categories and across apparel, accessories, and footwear.

TopShop has been increasing its footprint in the fitness category, as it faces competition from the likes of Athleta. So have its fast-fashion competitors, such as Uniqlo and H&M.

Other examples of celebrity deals in the fitness-plus-casual apparel space include Kate Hudson's ongoing line with Fabletics and Carrie Underwood's 2014 deal with Dick's Sporting Goods.

Alternatively, the licensee can bring the functional attribute to the deal. When Brookstone launched its Sleep Smart Bedding Collection, which was touted as anti-allergen, anti-static, and anti-moisture, it was the patented technologies of its two licensees, AQ Textiles and Design Weave, that offered these features. Similarly, Samsonite licensee Zee Co. brought travel-friendly qualities such as moisture-wicking and wrinkle- and tear-resistance to a line of Samsonite-licensed apparel.

Sometimes, rather than the licensor or licensee being the primary driver of the functionality, the licensor's brand positioning is simply a good fit with the licensee's capabilities.

London Luxury specializes in bedding such as mattresses, pillows, and box spring protectors that feature allergen-barrier fabrics, zipper and seam technologies, and other properties to protect against dust mites, pet dander, bed bugs, microbes, mold and mildew, and the like. It has secured licensing rights to logical properties such as Merck's allergy brand Claritin and the Terminex pest-extermination brand, as well as Arm & Hammer.

Often when a manufacturer or retailer expands its technical or performance offerings, it looks to a license to help with the launch. United Legwear wanted to add some performance properties to its products, such as moisture-protection, as these attributes became technically feasible, and turned to the Weatherproof brand as a good fit for the launch.

Similarly, as Kmart expanded its health and wellness offerings in the yoga, running, core training, and lifestyle categories in 2014 and highlighted technical attributes such as moisture wicking, quick drying, and reflective details, it paired with celebrity trainer Jillian Michaels. Adjmi Apparel Group division IFG produces the Impact by Jillian Michaels line.

Functional attributes extend beyond soft goods, of course. Everlast Worldwide licensed Cellutions LLC to produce its Everlast Hydrate Elite all-natural performance drink line. Its functional attributes include coconut water and sea salt, which help balance athetes' electrolytes.

No matter who brings the technical attributes to the party, the pairing of the property and product allows the traits to be logically integrated into the licensed line. And these attributes create a competitive advantage that goes beyond the lifestyle association that is often at the core of licensing deals, especially in apparel, accessories, and home goods.

Use of Ingredients, Materials, and Patented Technologies

In some cases where the licensor's brand is the driver of the functional or performance benefit, the licensor may sell ingredients or materials to the licensee as part of the deal. The decision of whether to include ingredients supplied by the licensor depends on a number of factors, including:
- The financial ramifications of including the ingredient (e.g. whether the licensee can do so profitably and/or what combination of ingredient sales versus trademark licensing revenue is most lucrative).

- Whether it is possible technically within the product category.

- Whether real ingredients bring a greater advantage to the product than other alternatives, either in measurable ways or in consumer perception.

- The importance of ingredient sales to the licensor's corporation as a whole.

The sale of ingredients and materials alongside trademark licensing deals occurs across industries.

Food: Companies such as Mars, with its M&Ms brand, or Mondelez International, with its Oreo brand, often participate in such agreements, both at retail and in food service. For example, J&J Snack Foods forged a deal with Mondelez to introduce Oreo Churros into food service channels. In these cases, the deal leans toward primarily an ingredient sale, with the trademark being licensed for use on packaging and in marketing. Typically, some sort of royalty payment is part of the deal, along with the payment for the ingredients themselves.

Most of these deals focus on mix-ins, such as candies or cookie pieces being includ-

Timberland Tires: Recycling in Action

One of the most complex licensing deals to date involving recycled materials—and an unusual one in the pairing of a truck tire and a fashion brand—is Timberland's partnership with Omni United to produce and manufacture a premium line of branded tires. The rubber used in the tires is specially formulated so it can be recycled optimally into shoe soles after the tires' automotive life is done.

Omni retained Liberty Tire Recycling to collect and sort the Timberland tires and make sure they are not mixed in with other brands during the recycling process. The crumb rubber will then be added to a compound that is appropriate for shoe and boot soles; the soles will be patterned to resemble a tire tread.

Although the first Timberland-branded tires will not be available for use in footwear until at least 2018, the specially designed boots are expected to launch in 2016 using recycled rubber from other sources. About 70% of Timberland's footwear already incorporates recycled or other eco-friendly materials, according to the company.

The tires, produced in the U.S. by Cooper Tire and Rubber and featuring Timberland's logo on the sidewall, are being sold in Omni's network of dealers and installers and promoted in Timberland's stores. The range of tires is expected to fit three-quarters of North America's passenger vehicles.

ed in cake mixes or ice cream. But occasionally ingredients will play a more integral role. The Welch's licensing program, for example, includes foods that feature real grape juice or jellies supplied by the company, as well as foods whose taste is inspired by these products.

Recycled products: Increasingly, merchandise marketed as ecologically beneficial incorporates recycled materials, a trend that began to take off in earnest in 2014. Celebrities such as Pharrell Williams, Lauren Conrad, and Will.i.am have all incorporated recycled materials into products tied to their names, as have brands including Coca-Cola and Timberland, among others.

Cannabis: A new and growing sector for ingredient licensing is cannabis. In 2014, several states made the use of marijuana legal for medical purposes and two (Colorado and Washington) for recreational purposes. This quickly led to the first uses of cannabis in licensed products such as drinks, candies, creams, and the like.

In some cases, the licensed product is associated with a particular brand of cannabis, the owner of which also supplies the ingredient. Canna Brands recently acquired Canna & Canna, a consumer goods company, to start developing branded cannabis-infused specialty goods such as bottled sodas, coffee beverages, and baked goods in states where they are legal. And Corr Products licensed its brand of marijuana, Green Rush, to a company called ID Global for use in nutraceutical energy drinks and ground coffee. Local companies in each state must be licensed to produce the products such companies develop, since neither marijuana nor products containing it can cross state lines.

External properties are also getting involved:
- Rockin Artwork was a pioneer in the field, licensing Cannabis Science, a medical marijuana developer, to feature Jimi Hendrix imagery in its branding and marketing in 2012.

- Relaxation Solutions, a subsidiary of BeBevCo, licensed Cheech and Chong for a line of hemp- and supplement-infused Relaxation Ice Cream under the Nice Dreams brand, inspired by the 1981 Cheech and Chong film.

- The estate of reggae artist Bob Marley launched a brand called Marley Natural, in partnership with Privateer Holdings, to market cannabis-infused lotions, creams, topicals, balms, and accessories.

Scented products: The incorporation of scent into products from apparel to stationery differs somewhat from other ingredient and material licensing in that the scent is often developed separately and reminiscent of the core brand, rather than being the core product itself or an ingredient used in the core product.

Candy brand Chupa Chups, which has a broad lifestyle licensing program, has increasingly been licensing scented products, from traditional categories such as air fresheners to newer opportunities such as scented pens. The tactic has become so frequent that it has developed a style guide for the proper use of scent in its licensed products. Cinnabon and Strawberry Shortcake are other properties for which scent has been a key component of many licensing iniatives, but the practice is expanding.

Springs Global, a bedding manufacturer, and Travelpro, a luggage and travel accessories company, acquired licensing rights to Febreze from Proctor & Gamble for lines of branded odor-eliminating products, working with micro-encapsulation company Celessence Technologies to develop the scent. And Barbie licensed apparel, featured as part of the Wildfox Resort 14 Dreamhouse Collection, includes items in which the fabric is sunscreen- or cotton candy-scented.

Made with...: A number of manufacturers have long-standing ingredient or material licensing programs in which the licensed product is identified as including or made with the material, rather than being branded. In these cases, the sale of the ingredient (and/or the licensing of a patent) is the primary business model, with the licensing of the trademark generating a small royalty on top of the revenues from the sale of the ingredient itself.

Examples include DuPont's Kevlar, 3M's Thinsulate, and Invista's Lycra brands. Ellery Homestyles, a marketer of home fashion products, markets ComfortTech blankets and SeasonSmart curtains that include 3M's Thinsulate insulation, for example, while Lycra has been licensed for a line of branded nail polishes in Europe, as well as granting royalty-free, non-exclusive licenses for apparel.

The number of programs of this sort is expanding. Honeywell recently announced that it would launch an official licensing program for Spectra brand fiber, which is used to make fishing line stronger. The initiative gives licensees the right to use genuine Spectra fiber (high molecular weight polyethylene) in their product and to market that fact, with a "Spectra by Honeywell" logo, as a means of differentiation. The company noted at the launch of the Spectra Brand Partner Program in 2014 that there have been more imitators over the years, some using names that play off the Spectra brand or falsely claiming to use Spectra in the product. Thus grew the decision to put an official licensing program in place. Honeywell's Advanced Fibers and Composites department drives the initiative.

As licensors and licensees are increasingly looking to add unique or superior functions to their licensed products to set them off from their competition, the inclusion of ingredients or materials as part of the deal is likely to become more common, where economically and technically feasible.

Ruggedness

One facet of the trend toward functional and high-performance licensed products consists of items that are rugged and durable. These products are intended for use in extreme conditions, such as outdoor construction work, in the military, or for outdoor sports and hunting and fishing.

Much of the activity is connected to workwear and workwear brands, which have been expanding their brand-extension and licensing activity and for which ruggedness on the job site is their core purpose. Many of their deals involve products that are touted as extra-rugged.

For example, Carhartt's licensees include Covercraft for duck seat protection using heavy-duty Carhartt fabric, meant for pickup trucks, vans, and other vehicles. Dickies and Walls, both owned by Williamson-Dickie, are also involved in outbound licensing (extensively, in the case of Dickies), as are other brands such as Wrangler Workwear. Meanwhile, these companies increasingly serve as licensees; Old Toledo Brands became a licensee for technical and casual fashions for the Rapala fishing lure brand in late 2014, for example.

Non-workwear brands also are looking for opportunities in rugged products; many of these licensors have strong associations with heavy-duty work or a rugged lifestyle:

- The nonprofit group Future Farmers of America (FFA) licensed the Ranchmate brand, known for its wire fencing-related products, for a co-branded line of work gloves intended for farming, ranching, fencing, and gardening.

- Survivalist and celebrity Bear Grylls partnered with Jivo Technology for a line of "ruggedized" electronic accessories that are dustproof and waterproof, as well as crush- and dropproof.

- National Geographic teamed with Live Prepared for a range of preparedness products for natural disasters, encompassing everything from shelter and first aid to energy, tools, and food prep.

- Scotts Miracle-Gro signed West Chester Protective Gear for lawn and garden gloves, along with a variety of other yard-work products, from lawn mowers to power tools.

- Coleman partnered with Ironclad Performance Wear for technical performance gloves designed for camping and outdoor sports, under both the "Built Tough by Ironclad" slogan and the Coleman branding.

- Caterpillar signed Bullitt Group for ruggedized cell phones that resist dust, can remain underwater for 30 minutes, operate when wet, and meet military spec requirements for shock, vibration, and temperature.

- Gas Monkey Garage authorized West Chester for welding caps and utility gloves.

Camouflage brands and designs play a role in the "ruggedness" sector, with camo patterns often incorporated into licensed products marketed by workwear, outdoors, and other rugged trademarks. The various camo brands, including Realtree and Mossy Oak, extend their brand names into a variety of rugged, outdoorsy products as well, in addition to granting rights for their camo designs.

Another facet of the trend toward ruggedness is the growth of the outdoors category in general for licensing, with an increase in deals having to do with camping, hunting, and fishing. Retailers such as Bass Pro, Gander Mountain, and Cabela's are also on the rise as purveyors of licensed merchandise, with artists such as Darrell Bush and the Hautman Bros. and country singers such as Luke Bryan among the types of properties that are increasingly active in this channel.

Everyday Function

The presence of licensing is on the rise in utilitarian categories where it did not have much of a role in the past or is being used in a new way. A number of factors are fueling the interest:
- Licensors of all types are looking for untapped categories where there is space for them to carve out a niche.

- Licensors with some sort of natural connection to utilitarian categories are entering the licensing business for the first time.

- Potential licensees in these categories have a growing awareness of and interest in licensing.

One arena that has experienced a significant amount of activity of late is cleanliness and trash disposal. In this case the growth is tied in part to the healthy-lifestyle and pro-environment trends that are so prominent in consumer products these days.

Household cleaning supplies have been a hotbed of licensing for several years, of course, thanks to cleaning product brands extending into closely related categories. Butler Home Products, for example, makes cleaning tools such as brooms, mops, and sponges under the Clorox, Dawn, and Mr. Clean licenses.

But property owners of other types, notably celebrities, are also becoming interested in the category. Martha Stewart launched a Martha Stewart Clean line of environmentally friendly detergents and household cleaners with Hain Celestial, while TV personality and interior designer Jennifer Adams developed a Whole House Cleaning Solution with Fizzion.

The trash bag category also has seen some movement. Church & Dwight signed Reynolds Consumer Products for a co-branded line of odor-neutralizing trash bags under the Arm & Hammer and Hefty names, while Waste Management, the trash-disposal service company, licensed Duro Bag and Reynolds for recycling bags and trash bags, respectively.

Other utilitarian product categories in which licensing is starting to emerge include:
- Paper towels (U.S. Army, NFL, Betty Boop in Turkey).

- Air filters (Lysol).

- Plumbing fixtures (Jason Wu).

- Office supplies such as printer paper (The Office, Kathy Davis).

- Mattresses (HGTV Home).

- Doors, windows, and cabinetry (Martha Stewart).

- Heating and hot water systems (Westinghouse).

None of these categories is entirely new to licensing; there is always room for properties with a good fit. But the amount of activity is growing and becoming more diverse.

4

A Top Priority: To Engage and Entertain

In 2014, the goal of engaging fans—creating a two-way conversation, developing a closer relationship, and/or fostering a deeper experience—became a higher priority for licensors and licensees. Some of the most-utilized techniques range from encouraging the creation of user-generated content, in all of its various forms, to offering experiential opportunities to strengthen the fans' connection with the brand.

Personalization And Contests: UGC At Its Simplest

User-generated content ranges from product customization to entirely original fan-created content or merchandise. IP owners deal with this phenomenon in various ways, sometimes by trying to control or guide the content, and sometimes by giving fans a wide berth, allowing them to drive the activity. The licensors monitor what is going on, with an eye toward potentially reacting or capitalizing.

The advantages of engaging fans through UGC extend beyond fostering loyalty and enthusiasm. Fan engagement also can have benefits in terms of concept testing and product development, for example. On the other hand, licensors face a continued battle between fostering fan engagement and protecting their intellectual content.

On the basic side of the UGC spectrum are ventures focusing on personalization and customization. To name just a few of many examples:

- Sites such as CaféPress or Shapeways allow users to create custom merchandise within the bounds of the licensor's rules. Fans use the assets provided, with the amount of customization varying by licensor and property.

- Retailer-specific initiatives bring people into stores and give them something unique that they had a hand in creating. Selfridge's partnered with Art You Grew Up With for a Mr. Men and Little Miss personalized art print pop-up shop.

- Licensee-driven ventures give fans of the product and property a chance to purchase something that stands out from the typical standardized mass-market merchandise. An example: My M&Ms Star Wars-themed candies, in which consumers could choose Star Wars-themed phrases and character imagery to imprint on their custom M&Ms chocolates.

The landscape of personalization and customization is becoming more diverse each day in terms of the properties, products, type of personalization, and service providers involved.

NFL fans can design exclusive products tied to Dallas Cowboys player DeMarco Murray through Fanprint.com, licensed by NFL Players Inc.; coffee lovers can have a different Cake Boss coffee flavor every day through a license between Discovery Communications and Single Cup Coffee; tweens can create One Direction mugs, cards, magnets, and t-shirts through PhotoBox Group sites, via a license with Global Merchandising Services; handbag lovers can customize the handbags they buy under the Deesigns by Dee Ocleppo brand on HSN; fans of Arsenal Football can create unique items in the personalization area at the club's megastore, operated with licensee PUMA; Merchant on Demand's Star Trek merchMAKER allows fans to select a product design, artwork, and their own Star Trek ship and rank, under license from CBS Consumer Products.

Contests are another mode of self-expression that falls on the simplest end of the user-generated content and fan-engagement spectrum. These initiatives encourage fans to create new content in a licensor-controlled environment for the chance to win a prize, often something like a publishing deal or wide distribution of their creation.

For example:

- In fall 2014, Lucasfilm offered a contest calling for fan-made films based on the *The Empire Strikes Back*, the second film in the Star Wars franchise. The best of 1,500-plus short films submitted, which were grouped into comedy, nonfiction, and animation categories, were posted on a YouTube channel, with winners' entries screened at the 2015 Star Wars Celebration fan event.

- Penguin Books ran a contest to solicit original novels tied to Jim Henson's classic film *Dark Crystal*, for a new young adult publishing program that launched in 2014. The winner, selected with input from fans as well as Penguin editorial staff, received a publishing contract for the first book in the series.

- NFL Players Inc. launched a competition for fans to submit ideas for toys aimed toward kids 8 and under that incorporate NFL players and related IP. Three finalists presented to a committee, with the winner's product being announced at Toy Fair 2015.

- Toys 'R' Us ran a "Turtles in Training" sweepstakes in conjunction with a line of exclusive Teenage Mutant Ninja Turtles toys, in which the winners receive a trip to Los Angeles to record a voiceover to be included in an episode of the TV series.

- American Greetings asked fans to create, submit, and vote on videos featuring Strawberry Shortcake and Care Bears, solicited through the Tongal creative community, with the winners used to promote the properties.

The number of similar initiatives has exploded in 2014 and 2015 and that promises to continue. The key will be to continually add new twists to make the initiatives stand out and give fans new ways to engage.

Utilizing the Crowd

Crowdsourcing combines fan creation and feedback and is increasingly being used to enhance licensors' and licensees' product development process, as well as to build and maintain fan excitement and loyalty. In fact, contests such as the ones mentioned above often involve crowdsourcing, in that fans are able to vote on their favorite entries as well as submitting their own content.

Some examples of ongoing crowdsourcing initiatives include:

- Cartoon Network, Ubisoft, and other licensors running contests with third-party crowdsourcing specialists such as Threadless and DesignbyHumans, in which fans create and vote on merchandise designs, with the winning entries being offered for purchase.

- Toy companies such as Mattel and LEGO overseeing open-innovation initiatives to give them direction on new products.

- Amazon launching a crowdsourcing platform, Kindle Worlds, for fan fiction submissions in the romance, sci fi/fantasy, and mystery/thriller genres, with winners getting an e-publishing contract. Hasbro is among the licensors experimenting with this platform. Individual publishers, such as Macmillan with its young adult

Swoon Reads platform, also are dipping their toes into crowdsourcing.

- Coca-Cola pairing with eYeka in China to solicit crowdsourced videos reflecting the taste of Coke, to be used as a type of market research as well as, potentially, marketing content.

Because of the simultaneous product development, exposure, and fan engagement benefits, crowdsourcing will certainly continue to grow. The means by which it is accomplished is likely to evolve as new technologies and new crowdsourcing platforms emerge.

Crowdfunding: Beyond Crowdsourcing

A more high-stakes version of crowdsourcing, which really came into its own in 2014, is crowdfunding. This technique involves marketers of licensed products soliciting funding from fans and potential consumers. Platforms such as Indiegogo and Kickstarter host the funding solicitations.

Incentives, such as the ability to receive the first products before they come on the market or participate in the creation of the product, are offered for different levels of funding. Shaquille O'Neal and Big Deez Productions turned to Indiegogo to generate $450,000 to finance the videogame *Shaq Fu: A Legend Reborn* on various gaming platforms. Some of the funding incentives included having the fan's likeness and name in the game, a variety of activities with Shaq, such as playing basketball at his home, and being present at the taping of one of the TNT NBA shows on which the athlete appears.

While the point of crowdfunding is ostensibly to raise funds, a more critical function in terms of licensed products is the ability to assess fan interest in the product as a whole and/or in various components of the product. While crowdsourcing does the same thing, fans' feedback tends to have more weight when accompanied by their money.

Strategic Crowdsourcing

Manufacturers, especially in the toy industry, are increasingly setting up ongoing review processes to allow fans to suggest and vote on new ideas for potential development into product lines.

The Lego Review, for example, is a competition in which users send in ideas for new Lego sets and vote on the best, with the winner being introduced into stores as a limited-edition Lego Ideas (formerly Lego Cuusoo) set. The 2014 introduction of the Research Institute, which features three female scientists, was a product of a Lego Review, as were several licensed examples, including Big Bang Theory and Dr. Who.

Some of the Lego Ideas sets, including licensed examples such as Minecraft, eventually transition into permanent product ranges.

In fact, most licensees typically have adequate funding to create and market licensed merchandise, or they would not have been granted a license in the first place (although at times the license is not final prior to the crowdfunding campaign).

In some cases the solicitation is positioned as being integral to the product being made, while in other cases it is clear that the item will become available no matter what, but that the funding will go toward additional bells and whistles:

- FarSight Studios crowdfunded a Star Trek: The Next Generation digital pinball game, using the money to pay the licensing fee, which it said would be financially unviable otherwise.

- NECA tried to raise funds for a Yu-Gi-Oh game card wallet, but did not raise the money and did not proceed with the product.

- Jasco Games planned to make a MegaMan board game whether it received funding or not; it used crowdfunding to test and pay for additional features.

It should be noted that most licensors are still wary of crowdfunding when it comes to products made by its licensees or prospective licensees. They are watching what happens and offering varying levels of support or permission (including none) to such ventures. Much of the activity is coming from product marketers who are associated or wish to be associated with a license that has a rabid fan base, often from the worlds of comic books, sci-fi, or similar entertainment.

Fan-Driven Initiatives

IP owners or their licensees have, to varying degrees, propelled the user-generated content sectors discussed so far. They have encouraged a two-way conversation with fans and fostered fan creativity, but all within the boundaries of their own rules.

Fans are independently originating a lot of content as well, however. For licensors, this is a positive trend in that it means fan loyalty is already strong and that their most loyal fans are communicating their love to others. This unsolicited and viral content expands awareness and strengthens the community as a whole. On the other hand, much user-generated content also violates the licensor's intellectual property rights.

Some key areas to watch when it comes to fan-driven content creation include:

- Products. Self-created room décor, craft projects, apparel, and other items featuring favorite characters are shared among fans on social media or in person, and sometimes sold through sites such as Etsy.

- Education. Teachers use favorite characters as the basis to create open-source lessons that fit their classroom curriculum. Probably the most active property tied to such activity as of early 2015 is Minecraft, which inherently has educational value.

- Fan fiction. As noted, companies such as Amazon and Macmillan have launched initiatives to formalize the fan fiction process, ensure IP laws are upheld, and mine fans' creativity for potential publishable stories. But fan fiction originated organically from readers and amateur writers wanting to create new stories based on their favorite properties, from Game of Thrones to One Direction.

- "Let's play" videos and "machinima." Videogamers create in-game "let's play" videos of their avatars making their way through games such as Super Mario Bros. or HALO, as well as "machinima," videos of original stories starring characters from popular games. Some of the most popular YouTube stars, such as PewDiePie and Stampy Longhead, come from this genre of user-generated content.

The result of all this activity is a balancing act in which licensors try to both maintain the fan engagement that is so valuable to the brand, while trying to uphold the integrity of the property by reining in the most flagrant violations. Licensors run the gamut from leaning heavily toward the trademark-policing end of the spectrum to being lenient and favoring fan engagement over trademark concerns (within reasonable limits).

Cartoon Network—which is on the latter end of the spectrum—saw its fans creating room décor and apparel based on its Adventure Time characters and used this information to spur product development. It realized there was a market for products and information that would appeal to crafters and signed PotterCraft for a book on DIY Adventure Time crafts.

Some licensors have gone so far as to help fans sell products they have created. In Japan, social media platform LINE oversees a licensing program based on its own characters, and secures rights to existing properties for purchasable stickers. Fans also create their own stickers. The company launched Line Creators Market to allow users to produce and sell their creations, after a review process, in the Line Store and the in-app Sticker Shop, receiving 50% of revenue. In a six-month period in 2014, more than 270,000 creators used the platform. Some users have created and sold other goods, beyond stickers, through the site as well.

Experiential Licensing and Promotion

It is no secret that experiential licensing—non-retail-product licensing deals that allow fans to interact with a property in a deeper way than with a traditional product—has been one of the fastest-growing areas of licensing over the past several years. Experiential licensing not only brings in revenues. It enhances fan engagement with and loyalty to a property and hopefully spurs continued fandom and consumer activity.

As Exhibit 3 shows, experiential licensing can take many forms, from services to entertainment to location-based initiatives. It occurs in all territories and involves nearly all types of properties. Some sectors, such as theme park attractions, restaurants, and retail locations, tend to involve the best established or hottest properties, or those owned by the biggest licensors, while others, such as touring stage shows,

Exhibit 3

Primary Sectors for Experiential Licensing

Type of Venture	Selected Examples
Restaurants	Three Stooges (with Legendary Burgers); Ford (with Ford's Garage); Minnesota Wild NHL team (with HMS Host for airport location); Harper's Bazaar (with Marka PJSC for café in the Middle East); PGA Tour (with HMS Host for airport grills).
Camps	FC Barcelona (soccer camps with Kaptiva Sports); Nike (with U.S. Sports Camps).
Theatrical productions	Geronimo Silton (with Susan Gurman Agency); Mister Maker (with Live Nation for Australia/New Zealand); Scooby Doo and Tom and Jerry (with Shooting Stars for the Middle East); Hunger Games (with Imagine Nation and Triangular Entertainment for permanent theatrical experience in London).
Location-based attractions	Thomas & Friends and other HIT brands (with Lappset for activity attractions); Top Gear (with Brandscape for a track experience); In the Night Garden (with Shanghai Yingbao for eduational play areas in China); NASCAR (with AMP Group for indoor kart racing facilities); SpongeBob and Dora (with The Little Gym for birthday experiences).
Services	Top Chef (with Blue Apron Media) for meal delivery promotion; Motor Trend (with Closet Factory for custom garage storage solutions); ELLE (with HowAboutWe.com for a matchmaking service).
Retail	Forbes (with Paradies for airport newsstands); Nickelodeon (with Entertainment Retail Enterprises for stores in global markets); Warner Bros. (with Exelixi Management for WB stores in India).
Education	Angry Birds (with 123 Education Development for curriculum in China); Dina Manzo (with Longevity's Party Planning Institute for online party-planning courses).
Tours & exhibits	Angry Birds (with Imagine Exhibitions and Jack Rouse Associates for science exhibits); Ice Age (with Premier Exhibitions for science exhibits); Skylanders (with GameTruck Licensing for nationwide mobile tour).
Travel	MasterChef (with Cox & Kings for culinary holidays and Life Journeys for cruises); New York Times (with four travel providers for land-based tours around the world); Discovery (with Princess Cruises).
Theme parks and theme park attractions	Nickelodeon (with Village Roadshow for attraction at Wet 'n' Wild in Australia and Parques Reunidos for a branded attraction in Madrid); Ferrari (with PortAventura Entertainment for a theme park in Barcelona); Universal (with Beijing Shouhuan for a theme park in China); Twentieth Century Fox (with Village Roadshow for a theme park in South Korea.)

Source: Raugust Communications

attract nearly any type of property. Services tend to involve properties with a defined niche or focused content, such as magazine brands.

Most experiential licensing is associated with some sort of royalty and therefore categorized as a licensing deal. But others take alternative forms, such as:

- A promotion (often the case with cruise or travel packages, such as the Seuss at Sea program on Carnival Cruises or the Tree Fu Tom-themed resort packages through travel operator Thomas Cook).

- A joint venture (often the case for theme parks, such as Shanghai Disney Resort, a partnership between Disney and the Shanghai Shendi Group).

- A licensor-owned venture (as with the Doc MacStuffins Check-Up Clinic retail tour or the Polaroid Fotobar retail chain).

- A franchise network (such as for retail or restaurant locations, such as Riki Group's 50 Smeshariki retail and entertainment centers in Russia).

Other configurations are possible as well.

One type of experiential licensing that has strengthened gradually over the past few years and saw a burst of activity in the second half of 2014 is the pop-up shop.

Pop-ups typically feature merchandise, often limited, personalizable, and/or exclusive, as well as a variety of activities, from celebrity appearances to interactive kiosks and beyond, depending on the nature of the property. Often set up in conjunction with a launch, anniversary, holiday, or other hook, they give fans an opportunity to get to know a property better and experience it in-depth. This is a benefit that is of primary importance, although publicity and some product sales often are secondary advantages.

Global Pop-Up Project

Korean fashion designer JuunJ, whose outerwear, sweaters, and other apparel items are available in limited distribution in 25 countries, launched 11 pop-up shops in eight countries for a two-month period in summer 2014. Locations included Opening Ceremony's New York store and similar shops in Paris, Tokyo, and other cities. The featured capsule collection was designed just for the venture, according to *WWD*, and included apparel such as sweaters and bomber jackets and accessories such as backpacks and caps (the latter from New Era). Artist Josh Luke, a U.S.-based sign painter, collaborated on the line, as well as on JuunJ's broader collection for fall 2014.

Properties launching pop-up shops in 2014 ranged from character/entertainment properties and social media platforms (AwesomenessTV, LINE) to designers, celebrities, and lifestyle brands (JuunJ, Goop, Paul Frank, Smiley). They are just as likely to occur in China (as was the case with UP Studios' BOOMi and BiBop pop-up) and other emerging territories as in Europe or the U.S.

Do-It-Yourself Fan Engagement

In some cases, traditional product categories can be a means of fan engagement as well. This is likely one of the factors behind the continued rise of crafting—as a product category, as a theme for entertainment productions, and as a retail channel for licensed products.

Even as consumers are creating their own content from scratch as outlined above, they also want guidance (e.g., patterns, ideas, instructions) from licensors and licensees to help them create their own handmade items featuring favorite characters. The act of creating is one way to gain a deeper experience with a property, whether a sports team, an artist, or a book character.

Crafts and crafting-based initiatives can take many forms:
- Properties of all types are entering the category. Fashion designer Isaac Mizrahi signed a deal with Michaels in late 2014 to exclusively distribute four yarn lines with 24 colors from licensee Premier Yarns, while Iconix signed a direct-to-retail deal with Walmart for its Waverly Inspiration brand for fabric and craft.

- Craft-based celebrities, including Katie Brown, host of a crafting series on PBS, and Lindy Smith, a U.K.-based sugarcraft artist, have extended their names into crafting items.

- Crafting brands, such as Crayola and Elmer's, continue to expand into not only arts and crafts, but home decor, cooking and baking, and other categories that allow children (and sometimes adults) to create DIY projects.

- Entertainment properties featuring crafting themes are launching, with examples from the U.S., Canada, and Britain including *Air Crafters, Trashionista, and iDoo-B-Doo.* They hope to emulate the success of properties such as the U.K.'s *Mister Maker*, which is well established and widely licensed.

- Broad licensed product lines include crafting as a component. Target's 25-piece girls' collection tied to the movie *Annie* included a DIY fashion-design kit.

While crafting is the most obvious fan-engagement category, there are other products that can satisfy the same objective, as well as bring in revenue. Interactive gaming, for example, helps solidify a fan's relationship with a property, just as a cruise or a pop-up shop can.

5 Telling a Story

Associating a property with a story—plotlines, character development, a world, a backstory—helps drive licensed product sales. This is not a new idea; it has long been almost a prerequisite for toys and many other products for kids. But the importance of story in these core categories has grown over time, and the concept has expanded into other property sectors as well. In fact, in 2014, *storytelling* became one of the top buzzwords in the licensing business.

The Story Behind The Toys

Toy companies were pioneers in this trend. They have long inserted mini-books or mini-comics into packaging and created original direct-to-DVD (now often direct-to-digitally distributed) programming to enhance play value. Those early initiatives have evolved into ever more sophisticated ventures, to the point that toy companies have become key players in entertainment creation. And the connection between toys and story-driven categories (entertainment, publishing, music) is stronger than ever.

Exhibit 4

Selected Entertainment Ventures of Toy Companies

Toy Company	Selected Entertainment Venture(s)
Colorforms	Purchased by TV producer/licensor Out of the Blue in 2014; new owner is developing apps and an animated series.
Fisher-Price	Working with HIT Entertainment (its sister company within Mattel) on a TV series based on its Little People toy brand.
Hasbro	Was in talks for a time to purchase film studio DreamWorks in 2014; has had successful film franchise for Transformers (with Paramount) and TV series for Transformers and My Little Pony. Also has extensive digital and print publishing programs across properties.
Jakks	Formed strategic partnership with Saban Brands to develop multi-platform property Emojiville, launching on digital platforms prior to TV series. Previously developed the Monsuno television franchise with Japanese production company Dentsu.
LEGO	Partnered with Cartoon Network to develop an original multiplatform property, the Mixels; creates online and TV animation based on its own and co-branded toy sets; was a pioneer in toy-entertainment field with Bionicles years ago.
Mattel	Launched Playground Productions, a division that will develop original multiplatform content including Team Hot Wheels: The Origin of Awesome and participate in film development including Max Steel. Has previously developed entertainment for brands including Barbie, Hot Wheels, Monster High.
MGA Entertainment	Developed Lalaloopsy TV series with Nickelodeon.
Moose Toys	Partnered with Nelvana to develop content based on Shopkins and Mutant Mania.

Exhibit 4 shows some of the recent steps toy companies have taken to develop their intellectual properties for entertainment across multiple platforms, including television, film, digitally-distributed content, gaming, and the like.

In some cases, these ventures are a matter of formalizing or taking more control of entertainment production activity that has been ongoing. Mattel has long had a program of original entertainment content tied to its properties, from its long-running series of Barbie original DVD productions to the newer Monster High and Ever After High brands. Both of the latter launched through books, toys, and digital content. In 2014, Mattel launched Playground Productions as an internal division to oversee this activity.

Similarly, Hasbro has long partnered with movie studios and television production and distribution companies to create entertainment content ranging from its series of Transformers films to its TV series tied to My Little Pony and Transformers. Its discussions about acquiring DreamWorks Animation, which became public and subsequently fell apart in late 2014, hinted at its desire to maintain more control over these ventures.

Other toy companies continue to forge alliances with outside partners rather than (or in addition to) developing story in-house. But they, too, are accelerating their entertainment production activity, as the exhibit shows. Spin-Master, Jakks Pacific, LEGO, and others are all taking steps to control and expand storytelling based on their brands.

Meanwhile, physical toy packages still feature content to add play value, and this content is becoming more complex. Rather than little booklets with simple stories being included in the box, there might be a series of exclusive comic books produced by the toymaker's retail comics licensee or a code to unlock high-quality digital entertainment productions available only to purchasers.

Bridging The Gap

Another development related to storytelling that has blossomed over the last decade is the creation of content to keep fans engaged between major entertainment releases. The proliferation of entertainment distribution channels—particularly digital platforms—has strengthened licensors' ability to disseminate such content and has solidified the continuous creation of content as a key strategy for entertainment licensors.

This type of content can satisfy audiences' craving for a property between significant releases, as is Disney's plan with its *Frozen Fever* short film in spring 2015. In other cases, the "bridge content" serves to fill audiences in on what happens to a character beyond or between films and TV series, as with Tor/Forge Books' three-novel series based on the Fox TV show *24*, released in 2014. Many sci-fi and interactive gaming properties have vibrant publishing programs to give fans another way, aside from the core entertainment, to participate in the world of the property.

In some cases, this content can even lend itself to limited licensed product initiatives. Disney has been involved in several such ventures. In the U.K., Disney created a Silver Series of die-cast vehicles from licensee Mattel and remote-controlled cars from Dickey Toys, both tied to an intermediate story arc based on the Cars film franchise, published in *Disney Pixar Cars* magazine.

Storytelling Beyond Entertainment

While its value is most obvious in connection with entertainment/character properties, the role of storytelling extends into other licensing arenas as well:

- In corporate licensing, companies such as Skechers have developed characters and transitioned into entertainment licensors, while maintaining their brand activity. Other corporate marketers have promoted their brand stories in more subtle ways, such as by creating cliffhanger TV ads to drive consumers to the web to see the conclusion of the story.

- In celebrity licensing, the story of the star's life, as told through social media, gossip media, and reality television, keeps consumers interested. Even in cases where celebrities are professionals such as chefs or interior designers—in which case their expertise is driving the product development more than their personal life—consumers get to know their stories. This helps keep the program fresh and cements brand loyalty.

- In sports, athletes tweeting about their personal lives or events that happened on the field of play can become viral and even lead to tie-in products, such as t-shirts featuring a phrase uttered on a basketball court or in a tweet. Sports properties and athletes also are creating television shows to connect story to sport and draw in young fans. LeBron James offered a YouTube-distributed animated series called *The LeBrons*.

- In fashion, consumers have become savvy about how design works and want to know more about the thought process designers have gone through to create new collections. In addition, designers' personal lives have become part of consumers' consciousness and help maintain brand awareness and even spur sales.

While the connection between story and sales of licensed merchandise is not as obvious as it is in the entertainment/character realm, all property types can benefit from a narrative element to enhance the brand and indirectly have a positive impact on sales.

Therefore, property owners of all types will increasingly promote brand stories—not marketing-driven scenarios but plotlines that are authentic and integral to the brand and mean something to consumers. They will do what they can to spur them to viral status, in the hopes that they will enhance the property's commercial success. Fostering social interaction, often centered on some sort of storyline, has become a key facet of licensed property marketing.

Platform Neutrality

For many years, the licensing community, especially on the entertainment/character side of things, has accepted that digital distribution was coming. But they were uncertain about when it would overtake traditional media as a means for consumers to experience entertainment. In addition, they wondered whether digital distribution, with its accompanying market fragmentation, would become a viable platform to launch a licensing program in the foreseeable future.

Some of these questions were answered in 2014, when digital distribution hit critical mass, rivaling or even overtaking traditional media for many consumers. Not only has it become commonplace for entertainment properties to secure distribution on Hulu, Netflix, Amazon Prime, or other digital distribution channels, but these platforms are viewed as being able to support existing licensing programs. They are even starting to emerge as viable platforms for new licensing initiatives.

Licensors have gone through a progression in how they view digital distribution. They began by looking to digital platforms for secondary distribution of existing properties, before moving on to create properties that were new for digital distribution but based on established franchises. Then they started creating digital-first properties that would debut on digital channels initially, with the idea that they would subsequently move into mainstream channels. (This step includes global properties using digital distribution as an introduction to a new territory before expanding to TV or film there.) Finally, they introduced all-original properties appropriate for digital-only distribution throughout their lifespans.

As Exhibit 5 shows, all of these strategies are in play today. Licensing programs have followed, even for some all-original properties. Most of the latter are limited in scope to date, but they have signed some licensees for core products.

Traditional television and film still lead when it comes to supporting storytelling around a licensing program, of course. Films create promotional opportunities and a buzz at retail; TV is still a key distribution venue, especially for certain consumer groups, such as preschoolers. But increasingly, licensors see the promise in platform neutrality, where consumers seek good entertainment from whatever distribution channel works for them. Fans want the entertainment to be available in the most convenient format, for use at a convenient time, and they view all distribution venues equally in terms of the quality of entertainment.

While this discussion and the exhibit focus on U.S. distribution deals, the same trend exists globally as well. For example, Disney has distributed its movies on Tencent, the top online movie service in China, while Amazon's European streaming service LOVEFiLM distributes properties from Disney, NBC/Universal, Saban, and other licensors. In fact, in countries such as China, many global and local licensors are using digital distribution to introduce and establish themselves.

Content Licensing for Multiple Touchpoints

With the almost insatiable consumer demand for content, along with the importance of story to propel demand for a property and its associated products, it follows that content licensing has become a major focus for entertainment licensors as a means to get their content out there in as many platforms as possible.

Exhibit 5

Key Strategies for Digital Distribution of Entertainment Properties

Type of Digital Distribution	Selected Examples	Typical Licensing Activity
Franchise-Based Original	DreamWorks' TurboFast and DinoTrux (Netflix); Mattel's Ever After High (Netflix); Disney and Lego's Lego Marvel Super Heroes: Maximum Overload (various); Rainbow's Winx Club WOW: World of Winx (Netflix); Mattel and WWE's WWE Slam City (various); HIT's Mike the Night movie (Hulu); Jim Henson's Doozers (Hulu); Saban's Popples (Netflix); 41 Entertainment's Kong: King of the Apes (Netflix); Lionsgate's Hunger Games: District Voices (YouTube); Scholastic's Magic School Bus 360 (Netflix); Guru's Justin Time The New Adventures (Netflix); American Greetings' Care Bears and Cousins (Netflix).	Varies depending on franchise activity; for example, book-based DinoTrux has none to date, WWE Slam City has a wide program, Winx has branded merchandise predating the online version.
All-Digital Original	Frederator's Bravest Warriors (YouTube/Cartoon Hangover); POW!'s Bad Days (YouTube/Stan Lee's World of Heroes); POW and Graphic India's Stan Lee's Chakra the Invincible (Rovio's ToonsTV); PBS's Plum's Landing (PBSKids.com).	Limited to date, with focus on books, comics, some collectibles.
Digital-First Original	Nickelodeon's Welcome to the Wayne (Nick.com); Disney's Sheriff Callie (WatchDisney app); PBS's Odd Squad (PBS Kids Online).	Typically limited until TV series airs.
Secondary Distribution	Scholastic with Netflix (Clifford, Magic School Bus library, other properties); Henson with Hulu Plus (Fraggle Rock, Mopatop's Shop, other properties); Steve Rotfeld Productions' Xploration Station with Hulu (airing immediately after broadcast on Fox TV stations); IMPS's Smurfs on YouTube.	May have merchandise on the market that predates digital distribution, depending on the age of the property and amount of time since last broadcast.
International Introduction	HIT's Fireman Sam (Amazon Prime); Imira's Lola & Virginia (Hulu); Ankama's Wakfu (Netflix); Sesame Workshop's Furchester (YouTube); Fuji TV's Ponkickies (Oznoz).	Typically limited; HIT's Fireman Sam deal includes merchandise on Amazon.

Note: There is overlap among sectors, with some deals including components of more than one category (e.g. Winx Club's deal with Netflix includes secondary distribution as well as the franchise-based original).
All-Digital Original = brand new property for digital-only distribution
Digital-First Original = new property that debuts on digital but has plans for traditional media
Secondary Distribution = property has aired already but gets a second life on digital distribution
International Introduction = debuts via digital distribution in new territory (U.S.) but has already aired in home country
Source: Raugust Communications

Content deals can take many forms:

- They can be accomplished through traditional licensing, through joint ventures, promotional deals, or some other configuration, or developed by the licensor in-house.

- They run the gamut from various digital platforms (Hulu, apps, virtual worlds, gaming) to traditional media (magazines, books), and beyond.

- They are heavily entertainment-based, but also involve other properties, such as interactive games starring Kim Kardashian or e-books featuring Coca-Cola advertising and design.

- They can be property-specific, such as a Peppa Pig magazine, Geronimo Stilton live stage shows, or The Hobbit interactive games; they can be co-branded, as when Dr. Who is featured in Minecraft: Xbox 360 Edition or Frozen is promoted within Club Penguin; or they can aggregate content from many sources, as the Speakaboos mobile educational platform does with content from HIT Entertainment, the Jim Henson Company, and Scholastic.

With the proliferation of platforms where consumers can enjoy entertainment and media, the market has become fragmented, a trend that promises to intensify as new platforms arrive on the scene. This means IP owners need to license or otherwise provide their content to a wide variety of platforms, or "multiple touchpoints." It also means that they need to have a continuous source of content that lends itself to a variety of platforms—interactive or analog, bite-size or long-form—and is fresh and new. For non-entertainment licensors, this means creating content from scratch; for entertainment licensors it typically includes a mix of existing content available in new forms and original content developed specifically for certain formats.

Meanwhile, the platforms for content licensing are proliferating beyond pure entertainment. Many licensors authorized content to be used in texting and chatting apps in 2014, for example. Companies such as LINE in Japan (and increasingly globally), WeChat in China, Kik in Canada, and Lango in the U.S. are among many such services to serve as licensees. They have acquired the rights to a variety of properties to be used as graphics—emoji or "stickers"—to convey various emotions or phrases in messaging. Aggregator/brokers such as meemo, TextPride, and Bare Tree Media have been established to serve this market, along with other social media venues.

Aside from texting, other social communications tools that have emerged as licensing platforms include:

- Branded email addresses. MyBrandEmail secured a license with Elvis Presley Enterprises for @allshookup.com.

- Licensed blogskins. Ameba Blog in Japan acquired the rights to imagery from artist Madeleine Floyd. Users can purchase such skins as a background look for their personal blogs.

- Photobombing apps. Paws and SocialIn partnered for Garfield photo packages within the PicsArt Photo Studio app, allowing characters to be added to selfies for sharing online.

Other segments, new and old, that need content include educational electronics and tablets for children, wearable electronics (e.g. weather information or calorie data for smartbands), virtual worlds, digital crafting sites and apps, digital Advent calendars, wedding planning and dating sites, fitness video content, and more.

6 Doing Well by Doing Good

The licensing community has long been talking about the viability of various types of pro-social, pro-environment, and pro-education initiatives, whether as a focus of a licensing deal or as part of a larger program. But while consumers say in surveys that such ventures make them more likely to purchase a product, that data has not historically translated to real-life purchasing. As a result, it has been difficult to create much enthusiasm among licensors, licensees, and retailers.

That said, 2014 was a watershed year in terms of the number of real initiatives that could be classified as "doing well by doing good." And each instance of success will help build a track record that should propel this trend forward in the coming years.

Saving the Environment

Licensing deals that attempt to minimize harm to the environment comprised one area of growth in 2014, for a number of reasons:

- Technology has made it possible for recycled materials to be used effectively in both soft and hard goods, leading to products that are fashionable and visually appealing, as well as ecologically sound.

- Price differentials between pro-environmental and traditional products are declining, lowering one of the key barriers between intent to purchase and actual purchase.

- Bad news about the environment and growing public acceptance of the existence of global warming combined to add an incentive to buy such products.

- Celebrities often consider the environment to be one of their causes and insist on incorporating ecologically sound attributes into their product lines. With the continuing expansion of celebrity licensing comes the expansion of eco-friendly licensed products—and potentially more consumer demand.

In fact, as the handful of examples in Exhibit 6 shows, many of the highest-profile ventures involving recycling and organic materials are tied to celebrities, although corporate brands are part of the mix as well; the Timberland tire branding and recycling program discussed in detail in Chapter 3 is one example.

Made In....

Another topic that has been a matter of discussion in the licensing business for a long time is the value of a "made in America" positioning. It has been mostly talk until 2014, however. Like pro-environmental characteristics, domestic manufacturing is something that consumers claim they want, but they tend to be slow to put their money into it. This is particularly true when U.S.-made products command a price premium over foreign-made.

In 2014 (and likely in the years to come), prices are coming down for U.S.-made products, thanks to technology innovations and other factors. At the same time, costs related to Asian-made products are rising, due in part to higher salaries in key manufacturing countries. Therefore, the price differential between made-in-America and foreign-made products has narrowed.

In addition, memories of the Great Recession are fresh and employment rates continue to lag behind other economic measures during the recovery. These factors, along with more viable pricing, has made it possible for retailers and manufacturers to expand their focus on U.S.-made products, and for U.S. consumers to feel good about buying them.

In 2014, Walmart was in the 10th year of its long-term initiative to source more products from U.S. factories, with the value of its purchasing estimated at $50 billion that year and the cumulative value over the next decade forecasted to be $250 billion. Its support of "made in America" has been a key driver of this trend within the licensing business.

Exhibit 6

Selected Pro-Environmental Initiatives With Licensing Connections

Property	Eco-Friendly Initiative
Lauren Conrad	Launched the XO(eco) brand for products featuring REPREVE fabric made from recycled plastic bottles. Licensees including Blue Avocado (travel and storage accessories) sell at Kohl's, exclusive retailer of Conrad's LC Lauren Conrad apparel line, and other retailers.
Pharrell Williams	Launched Bionic Yarn in partnership with Parley for the Oceans. Company turns trash found in the ocean into fabric, which is then used in products, including Williams' collaborations with G-Star and Adidas.
Stella McCartney	Participated in Fashion Positive, an initiative from Cradle to Cradle Products Innovation Institute, along with other fashion labels, to create a capsule collection using suppliers approved by Cradle to Cradle. All of the suppliers are authorized for making a positive environmental and social impact.
TerraCycle	Allies with consumer brands, which agree to send used packaging to TerraCycle, which in turn designs new items incorporating the waste and licenses manufacturers to produce items such as tote bags and scrapbooks. The packaging is used in its entirety (e.g. a tote made from drink packages), so the consumer brand is prominently displayed.
Timberland	Launched tire branding and recycling program with Omni in which Timberland branded tires are specially configured to be recycled after use into Timberland shoes. A chain of custody process includes collection points, recyclers, and rubber processors.
Waste Management	Licensed Duro Bag Manufacturing for a line of branded recycling bags with graphics illustrating which household items can be recycled.
Will.i.am	Partnered with Coca-Cola for Ekocycle brand. Licensees including Beats (headphones), Levi's (denim), H. Brothers (men's suits), Case-Mate (smartphone cases), and New Era (caps) create limited edition products made partially of recycled Coca-Cola bottles.

Source: Raugust Communications

Licensors of outdoors-related properties from Remington to Duck Dynasty often look for opportunities for made-in-U.S. licensed goods where economically feasible (although this is not the primary consideration for licensee selection in most cases).

The fashion industry is focused on American-made products as well. Lucky Brand launched a capsule collection with U.S.-based Cone Mills for denim that is domestically produced, cut, and sewn, and Filson partnered with Shinola for a U.S.-made watch collection, to name just two of many examples.

In addition, more licensees are touting the fact that their licensed goods are U.S.-made. Realtree licensee Carhartt promotes its position as the camo brand's only line of apparel made in the U.S.

This focus on domestic manufacturing is not limited to the U.S. The global recession, among other factors, has spurred similar initiatives in places such as the U.K., France, Italy, and Germany.

The nature of these programs varies. They can be:
- Led by licensors, as with designer Vivienne Westwood's series of collaborations with U.K. firms for British-made goods.

- Driven by industry groups, as in Italy.

- Promoted by the government, as in France.

- A result of the collective efforts of individual manufacturers working independently, as in Germany.

The trend should expand globally as additional countries, especially China and other Asian territories, are strengthening their support of domestic products. Many governments are trying to convince their consumers that local goods are of equal or superior quality to the foreign products they tend to prefer.

Worker's Rights

The rights and safety of workers who produce licensed products is another pro-social issue that has been around for a long time but seems to be intensifying and/or gaining a higher profile.

Events such as the lethal factory fire in a Dhaka industrial district in Bangladesh in November 2012, which killed more than 100 workers and injured 200 others, raised public awareness about this issue. It led manufacturers and retailers to take additional steps—while stressing that they already had strong procedures in place—to protect workers and ensure that their products are not causing harm.

The most common procedure is for licensors, retailers, and licensees to sign on with one of the industry groups that have agreed to monitor worker conditions and ensure that foreign companies do not contract with dangerous factories. Licensors require their licensees to sign a legally binding contract stating that they will use only factories authorized by either the European-centric Accord on Fire and Building Safety in Bangladesh or the U.S.-led Alliance for Bangladesh Worker Safety.

The Marine Corps' licensing office is one of many property owners that put higher standards in place for its licensed products, signing on with the European group. One of its products was found in the burned factory in Bangladesh.

Colleges tend to be at the forefront of this trend, thanks in part to pressure from their students and alumni.

In the spring of 2014, the University of Wisconsin-Madison began requiring its licensees that had products manufactured in Bangladesh—21 of its almost 450 total licensees at the time—to sign the Accord on Fire and Building Safety. Licensees including Adidas, Cutter & Buck, and Russell, among others, either signed or already were members of the group. Like other universities, UW already has a code of conduct, supplied by its agent the Collegiate Licensing Company and monitored by the independent Workers Rights Consortium, with which its licensees must comply.

Similarly, as of early 2015, the University of North Carolina is undergoing a review of its licensing process and its licensees, including VF Corporation, which works with several factories in Bangladesh. Student activist groups have been pressuring for change, particularly with regard to VF, which as of late November had not signed on to the Accord on Fire and Building Safety.

Licensees have had their contracts terminated due to noncompliance with such requirements. Rutgers canceled deals with Outdoor Cap and VF Corporation subsidiary Jansport in mid-2014 due to their refusal to sign the Accord. The former said it did business in Bangladesh but believed its internal processes for protecting workers was adequate, while Jansport said it did not produce in Bangladesh, although its parent did.

Aside from factory conditions, other social issues being monitored by licensors, often thanks to consumer pressure, include child labor and payment issues. H&M banned an Indian company, Super Spinning, from supplying yarn to any of its vendors, due to child labor and other violations.

And the closure of the PT Kizone factory in Indonesia in 2011 later caused troubles for Adidas, which sourced products from it. Eight of the universities Adidas worked with demanded that it pay severance to the 2,800 workers who lost their jobs in the closure and did not receive such pay from the factory.

Health and Wellness

The health and wellness sector also took off in earnest in 2014, after many years of slow growth in both interest and licensing activity. This trend is quickly becoming much more evident across a wide variety of property types and product categories, with various permutations.

To help combat obesity among young people, children's properties have participated in promotions around the globe to encourage kids to eat more fruits and vegetables. Examples include Sesame Street and The World of Eric Carle in the U.S., LazyTown in Hungary, and Moshi Monsters in the U.K. Licensors such as Disney, Warner Bros., and Viacom International authorize branded fresh produce in various territories.

Children's properties are also becoming involved with fitness-themed educational and activity initiatives. eOne has partnered with tumuv for a "Move with Peppa Pig" physical activity program for preschoolers launching in youth activity centers in the U.K. in 2015. Turner Broadcasting has teamed with Urban Legacies in a global deal to introduce LazyTown-themed activity attractions featuring child care areas, merchandise stores, and a café. And Saban has allied with Fit for Sport for a fitness guide distributed through schools and camps.

Disney's Marvel characters represent one illustration of the child-directed fitness licensing trend. It has upped its activity in all kinds of health and wellness products, including sports performance apparel with Under Armour, electronic fitness accessories with Tantrum, bike accessories and helmets with Bell and C-Preme, respectively, and Sage Fruit for produce.

For adults, a variety of fitness properties are expanding their brands into exercise apparel and equipment, foods, and other healthy items, through both licensing and other collaborative arrangements. Examples include fitness centers (Bally Total Fitness, Pure Barre), TV shows (*Biggest Loser*), magazines (*Cooking Light, SELF*), fitness celebrities (Jillian Michaels, Tracy Anderson), multimedia brands (BeFit, Veria Living), and sports properties (Bellator MMA, England Rugby, colleges, the major U.S. sports leagues).

Meanwhile, licensing is growing as a factor in a number of health-related categories. These include nutritional supplements with celebrities such as Martha Stewart, Arnold Schwarzenegger, Mark Wahlberg, and Flo-Rida and sports properties such as Manchester United (in China); coconut water (which promotes hydration during exercise) with Everlast and Jamba Juice; antimicrobial bedding with brands such as Arm & Hammer, SELF, and Terminex; and wearable fitness trackers with Tory Burch, Skechers, and Swarovski.

Retailers also are getting into the act—both with organic products and better-for-you products in general—pairing with licensed properties for health-related programs. Walmart is one chain that introduced the Wild Oats brand (formerly a health food retailer) in its stores with 100-plus natural and organic foods, while 7-11 tested a line of fresh and nutritional sandwiches, salads, and juices with fitness expert Tony Horton, known for his DVD workout series, in Southern California.

This list represents just a small sampling of the diversity of deals that are being done in the health and wellness category. While not all will be successful, most licensing executives believe the fundamental trend of health and wellness will be a key driving force across the entire licensing business going forward.

Education Gaining STEAM

While educational products have long represented a niche in the licensing business, activity in this segment is increasing in many ways. The trend is evident in the development of children's entertainment properties; in the use of licensing for educational products, content, and services; and in the distribution of content and merchandise into schools, libraries, and youth centers.

Much of the focus when it comes to property development has been on STEM (Science, Technology, Engineering, and Mathematics) and, more recently, STEAM (which adds Art to the other four disciplines). Edutainment properties, both digital and traditional, also are focusing on subjects and pedagogy that are integral to the recently introduced (and controversial) Common Core curriculum adopted by many U.S. states.

Exhibit 7

Selected Children's Properties with STEM and STEAM Themes

Property/Licensor	Description	Distribution and Licensing
Doozers/ Jim Henson Company	Preschool spin-off of Fraggle Rock that focuses on "design thinking."	Distributed on Hulu as its first original property. Simon & Schuster is among initial licensees, for books.
George Greenby/ Nerd Corps	Series based on the book series by Stephen Hawking and daughter Lucy Hawking, with physics themes.	In development.
Peg + Cat/ Fred Rogers Company	Math-focused preschool series starring a girl, with math-themed visual elements throughout.	Airs on PBS Kids; Candlewick is among the first licensees, for books, with HiHat Media signed as U.S. licensing agent.
Thomas Edison's Secret Lab/ Genius Brands	2D animated series produced with Georgia Public Television, set to debut in 2015.	Premiering on public television stations in April 2015; no licensees at press time, but plans in place for toys, apps, games, electronics, and in-school curriculum.
Numtum Adventures/ BBC Worldwide	Math-focused series targeted at older end of the preschool market.	On Cbeebies in the U.K.; no products available as of presstime.
BLAZE/Nickelodeon	Monster truck-focused preschool series with themes including all STEM subjects.	Airs on Nick Jr.; licensees include Random House for books; full range of products to launch in 2015.
Team Umizoomi/ Nickelodeon	Established preschool series with math themes.	Airs on Nick Jr.; range of licensed products from Jay Franco, Random House, Crayola and others launched in 2011.
Magic School Bus 360/Scholastic	Relaunch of the classic series for elementary ages as a multiplatform property.	Airing on Netflix starting in 2016; Scholastic publishes books, with more licensing planned. Products such as science kits are still on the market.
Xploration Station/ Steve Rotfeld Productions	Programming block on Fox consisting of four STEM-themed shows, each with a different celebrity host. Topics include space, animal science, marine biology, and emerging technology.	Airs on Fox TV Saturday mornings; no licensing at press time.

Source: Raugust Communications

As Exhibit 7 shows, target audiences for educational properties range from pre-school through tween/teens (with preschoolers the most common group). Girls are often a particular focus, with the main character or a strong secondary character being an independent-thinking female.

Aside from STEM and STEAM, other educational topics are popping up as well. Studio 100 is producing a program called *Knietzsche* that focuses on philosophy; PBS Kids' *Fizzy's Lunch Lab* and the independent *NutriVentures*: *The Quest for the Seven Kingdoms*, both online-distributed, focus on nutrition; and Genius Brands' *The Secret Millionaire's Club* with Warren Buffet emphasizes financial literacy. The last has been around for several years but is expanding its licensing activities in 2015.

Traditionally, educationally themed television programming has been a difficult sell for licensing, competing against the Disneys of the world for shelf space and with products being more attractive to parents than children. As a result, many of these programs' plans for merchandise remain fairly limited, focusing on logical categories such as print and digital publishing and apps, science and activity kits, other educational toys and electronics, and experiential and curricular ventures.

Exhibit 8

Educational Initiatives With Growing Licensing Activity

Type of Initiative	Examples	Selected Licensed Properties Involved
Curriculum	Curriculum for all ages, ranging from educational units for preschools to for-credit offline and online classes for adults, to massively open online courses (MOOCs), to language-learning courses for various ages and distribution channels. Some are commercial, others supported by nonprofit groups.	World of Eric Carle, Minecraft, NASCAR, Pocoyo, Sesame Street, Bill Nye, PEEP and the Big Wide World, Smithsonian
Classroom supplemental materials	Workbooks, flash cards, posters, etc. for classroom use, sold to teachers through teacher stores, online, and at retail. Consumers also can purchase.	World of Eric Carle, Guinness World Records.
Experiential ventures	Science-themed permanent or touring exhibits for malls, museums, and classrooms; science-themed "experiences" and shows, often but not always for classrooms.	Ice Age, Thomas & Friends, Angry Birds.
Content licensing	Content provided for apps, dedicated children's tablets, and other educational platforms.	Sprout properties, PBS Kids-distributed properties, Garfield.

Source: Raugust Communications

But several trends indicate that educational properties may have a greater likelihood of success today than in the past:

- Key players, which already command shelf space and a certain level of power with retailers, are becoming involved. Nickelodeon's BLAZE—which has the advantage of featuring ever-popular monster trucks as well as educational themes—has plans for products across categories, not just in the education space.

- Exposure through schools, after-school programs, and other similar settings (e.g., via curriculum programs) is increasingly recognized as a strong addition to television or online distribution as a means of exposure and awareness.

- The development processes for educational shows increasingly tend to balance entertainment and engagement equally with educational themes. This suggests children are more likely to watch because of the humor, stories, or interactivity, despite their traditional aversion to educational TV.

- The licensing community, from manufacturers to licensors and agents to retailers, are increasingly interested in becoming involved with such properties, although most continue to have mostly specialty rather than mass potential.

- Retailers such as Barnes & Noble and Toys 'R' Us are increasing shelf space devoted to educational products.

- Most importantly, there are indications that consumers are demanding such themes. LEGO's addition of a girl-centric SKU called The Research Institute was the result of its ongoing LEGO Review crowdsourcing process, meaning consumers spurred and supported the idea upfront.

In addition to the proliferation of educationally themed entertainment properties with licensing viability, other licensing trends include the rise of curriculum and supplemental materials, the licensing of content for tablets and apps, and experiential initiatives involving a variety of properties, educational and otherwise.

As Exhibit 8 shows, the supplemental materials, content, and experiential sides of things tend to mostly be directed at children and often focus on science themes (especially when it comes to exhibits), while the curriculum sector is much more diverse, ranging from educational units distributed through preschools, to online educational initiatives that can be used in schools or at home, to adult-targeted college-level courses involving a variety of academic and professional subjects.

It should be noted that some educational initiatives are not necessarily officially licensed. Certain properties lend themselves to education and are popular with children and, as a result, teachers (or even parents or the students themselves) sometimes create curriculum or learning aids featuring those properties.

Minecraft is one property that teachers have used in this way. Minecraft owner Mojang (now owned by Microsoft) has a division called MinecraftEDU that provides copies of the games for classrooms, but teacher-generated content is a separate and vibrant driver of Minecraft educational usage.

Feeling Charitable

The idea of including some sort of cause-related overlay, usually a percentage of sales or flat donation to a cause, as part of a licensing agreement—especially around holidays or in conjunction with key events such as anniversaries—is nothing new. But the incidence of such techniques is growing, especially when it comes to ventures occurring throughout the year, beyond holiday periods or events.

Charitable tie-ins and overlays extend across a variety of property types, product categories, retail partners, and types of causes. A few examples illustrate some common techniques:

•   Celebrity foundations: Musician Shakira's income from her deal with Fisher-Price for the co-developed First Steps Collection of developmental toys goes to her Barefoot Foundation, which promotes childhood development initiatives in Latin America.

•   Holiday tie-ins: Paul Frank's New York pop-up shop during the 2014 holiday season included a tie-in with Covenant House, which aids the homeless in that city. Visitors to the shop could make donations or purchase a pair of Paul Frank pajamas to donate and get 50% off their own PJ purchase in return. Paul Frank also made a straight donation of money and pajamas to the group.

•   Dedicated collections: Twenty-five percent of the retail price of each celebrity designer three-pack from baby brand aden + anais in 2014 went to the AIDS charity (RED). The packs, designed specifically for this program, included three organic swaddles featuring custom prints designed by Jessica Alba, Gwen Stefani, and Rachel Zoe.

These examples just touch the surface of the varied types of charity overlays that are proliferating as part of licensing deals.

It should be noted that the prevalence of cause marketing tie-ins as part of licensing

Charity Tie-Ins and Retail Exclusives

Retail-exclusive promotions and product lines highlighting licensed properties often have a charity overlay of some sort, as these examples suggest:
• Ten percent of sales on a collection of Moomin apparel at Scandinavian retailer Lindex, specially designed to mark the 100th anniversary of creator Tove Jansson's birth, went to Unicef to support children's education and literacy.
• Twenty-five percent of sales on a limited-edition gift line that was part of Barneys' Baz Dazzled holiday campaign in 2014, done in conjunction with film director Baz Luhrmann and his wife, costume designer Catherine Martin, went to Room to Read, an organization promoting literacy and gender equality in education globally.
• One percent of total sales of PBS Kids' exclusive toy line at Whole Foods Market, up to $25,000, goes to the Whole Kids Foundation, which supports nutrition and wellness. As always, all of PBS Kids' revenues will go toward the nonprofit's programming and other initiatives.

efforts throughout the year results in challenges for nonprofit licensing programs. Traditionally, nonprofits have faced an uphill battle in trying to sign licensees and secure retail space, since they are competing against branded and licensed products tied to strong properties and trademarks. The main differentiator they could present to potential partners, and to consumers, was that product purchases would support their cause.

Now, however, with so many licensing ventures including a cause overlay, whether through one of the partners' own foundations or a charitable partner, the inherent advantage possessed by nonprofit licensors is not as desirable as it has been in the past. Although they may be involved in such ventures as the recipient of the funds generated, their own licensing programs are more difficult than ever.

7

Power of Two

These days, two brands or properties are better than one. Pairing like or unlike properties brings additional credibility and interest. It offers something new to devotees of both, and potentially encourages fans of one to cross over and become fans of the other.

Three techniques have emerged as frequent means of doubling the power of a licensing deal: cross-licensing, co-branding, and collaborations. Meanwhile, retail-to-retail alliances, accomplished through licensing or some other form of partnership, continue to multiply.

The Three Cs

Exhibit 9 outlines the differences between cross-licensing, co-branding, and collaborations, with examples of each. The small sample shows the diversity of the market in terms of type of deal, property types involved, and geographic regions covered.

Exhibit 9

Partnership Power: Collaborations, Cross-Licensing, and Co-Branding

Type of Deal	Definition/ Characteristics	Typical Partners	Examples
Cross-licensing	Two intellectual property owners band together to create a licensing program, with the licensors jointly authorizing a group of manufacturers to market products featuring both properties.	Often character and/or sports licensors, but most property types are represented. Properties can be like (character x character) or unlike (sports x character).	Care Bears x Bunny King, Betty Boop x Chupa Chups, Tokidoki x Major League Baseball, KISS x Uglydoll, Nameko Sabai x Hello Kitty, Smeshariki x Zenir St. Petersburg, NCAA/colleges x Kellogg's characters.
Co-branding	A licensor's brand or property and a licensee's brand are featured on a single product.	Sports leagues and sports apparel brands, food ingredient purveyors and other food brands, character properties and mobile app/virtual world brands, characters or sports and fashion retail brands, entertainment properties and toy construction kits, others.	Neon Genesis Evangelion x Puzzle & Dragons, Miffy x 2 Percent, SpongeBob x Sprayground, Pokemon x Beams, Paddington x Om Nom, Star Wars x Minecraft, FIFA World Cup x Monopoly, Starburst x Rita's Italian Ice.
Collaboration	The creation of a brand-new product line through the involvement of two partners.	Often fashion labels, retailers, celebrities, musicians, or artists, but almost any property can be involved.	Lauren Moshi x DC Comics/Looney Tunes, M.I.A. x Versace, Mountain Dew x Atiba Jefferson, Playboy x Hysteric Glamour, Junya Watanabe x Loewe, Topshop x Kate Moss, Neff x Wiz Khalifa, Rick Owens x Selfridges, Alexa Chung x AG Adriano Goldschmied, Disney x Satya Paul.

Note: These sectors overlap, with some deals having characteristics of more than one; there is a particular blurring between co-branding and collaboration.
Also, the terms are often used interchangeably.

Source: Raugust Communications

In some cases the differences among the three classifications are subtle. There is some overlap, and the terms are often used interchangeably. In particular, the term *co-branding* is used by many to refer to ventures that fall into all three of the realms discussed here, since both partners' brands or property names typically appear on products or packaging; cross-licensing and collaboration are two forms of co-branding in this broader sense.

Licensors across all segments utilize all three techniques, although each tends to be more common among certain property types, as the exhibit indicates. In terms of product categories, apparel and accessories are core to most of these ventures, but other product categories, such as home goods, interactive games, and toys, can be the focus as well.

The power of partnership has been one of the factors driving retail collections involving all kinds of celebrities. Many of these personalities have little or no history or credibility in design or licensing, but pairing with a strong brand, especially in a short-term deal, allows them to dip a toe into the market with relatively low risk.

For example, Hayden Christensen, a young actor best known for his role in the more recent *Star Wars* films, collaborated with Canadian fashion label RW&CO on a 20-piece menswear capsule in 2013 under the Christensen for RW&CO label. It was available in stores across Canada, where the actor was born. This type of deal would have been almost inconceivable a decade ago—Christensen's fame is not among the top tier of celebrities and his fashion design experience was nil—but has become common today.

Many ventures in all three partnership classifications tend to be limited editions and/or capsule collections; these techniques are discussed in more depth in Chapter 12.

At some point the pendulum may swing back, but with the current competitive conditions at retail and in licensing, cross-licensing, co-branding, and collaboration should continue to maintain their prominent role within the licensing business in the foreseeable future.

Partnership as Strategy

While the types of initiatives discussed here were initially viewed as a way to stand out from the competition, they quickly evolved into standard operating procedure. While they are no longer unique, they still add some excitement and generate publicity for the properties involved.

Many IPs these days celebrate events such as anniversaries or the premiere of a film with multiple collaborations, usually short term in nature. Corporate brands such as Mustang and Playboy partnered with multiple designers to celebrate milestone birthdays in 2014, for example. Ford's Mustang program involved designers including Anna Sui, Rogan, CO|TE, Pamela Love, and Paula Cademartori.

Disney's *Malificent* was one of several 2014 films to offer a range of designer collections as a means of promoting the movie. Stella McCartney was one featured collaborator. And Mattel's Barbie introduced fashion collaborations with a number of retail brands, including Forever 21, Uniqlo, Primark, and Lord & Taylor, each aiming toward a specific demographic group or geographic territory.

While shorter-term initiatives are common when it comes to cross-licensing, co-branding, and collaboration, some licensors and retailers have made these sorts of partnerships a core strategy, either embarking on one venture for the long term or, more frequently, running a series of separate collaborations one after the other. Fast fashion, discussed in more depth in Chapter 2, is emblematic of such a strategy. Retailers such as Target, H&M, Kohl's, Uniqlo, and others offer their customers a continuous string of collections with different designers (or other properties). The major home shopping networks, HSN and QVC, follow a similar path.

A variety of property owners also have made such partnerships a key component of their licensing strategy. Fashion labels such as Jason Wu, Karl Lagerfeld, Alexander Wang, and others have tied in with multiple retailers and product partners over time, as have non-fashion-related properties such as Hello Kitty, The Simpsons, KISS, Uglydoll, Tokidoki, Chup Chups, Domo, Star Wars, DC Comics, the four major U.S. sports leagues, and many more.

Global Participation

Licensing ventures involving multiple properties or brands occur in all territories, from the newest to the most mature. The North American, Western European, and Asian markets, not surprisingly, are the focus of the greatest number of initiatives.

Within Asia, Japan and Hong Kong have been particularly strong markets for cross-licensing, co-branding, and collaboration, with mainland China not far behind. Hello Kitty alone has paired with a number of properties that share its Japanese heritage, including New Japan Pro-Wrestling, interactive gaming property Nameko Sabai, artist Shinzi Katoh, and anime property One Piece, to name a few. Many of these collections have been available on a global basis.

Meanwhile, Japanese design labels including Hysteric Glamour, Beams, Nigo/Human Made, Junya Watanabe, and Ropé Picnic are among the many that have collaborated with brands, characters, and other properties, both at home and abroad.

Although mature regions naturally are where most of the action is, emerging licensing territories have not been left out of the trend. Disney worked with Indian designer label Satya Paul on a collection of saris tied to Minnie Mouse under the Minnie Mono Pop brand, while Pepsi highlighted Ukrainian designer Masha Reva as part of a global program involving young designers around the world.

Exhibit 10

Selected Retail-to-Retail Partnerships

Host Retailer	Guest Retailer	Description of Venture
Macy's	LIDS Sports Group	Locker Room by Lids departments piloted in 25 Macy's stores in 2013, rolling out to 175 in 2014. Departments contain licensed sports league and collegiate apparel, headwear, and home goods.
Claire's	Dylan's Candy Bar	Dylan's Candy Bar-branded jewelry, nail and lip products, and tech accessories available exclusively at Claire's (and Dylan's locations) starting early 2013.
Walmart	Wild Oats	Defunct natural/organic retailer's brand relaunched in early 2014 on a line of 100-plus foods, from quinoa to salsa. Fresh & Easy supermarkets in Southwest U.S. have a similar deal with Wild Oats.
Toys 'R' Us	Claire's	Claire's branded shops in 12 U.S. and 100 European TRU stores as of 2014, after a successful test in Europe. Products similar to traditional Claire's assortment; size of shop varies by location.
Mariano's	Crumbs Bake Shop	Test of snack bar featuring 25 cupcake and 15 brownie flavors, in a suburban Chicago supermarket. Crumbs standalone shops had closed after bankruptcy.
Sears	James Allen	Exclusive jewelry boutiques at 16 Sears locations in two states and Puerto Rico. Boutiques within jewelry departments feature 120 styles plus online-only options.

Source: Raugust Communications

Retail Plus Retail

As early as 2010, retailers began to believe that they could license their names and in-house brands for merchandise to be sold in other retail settings. Sears made its DieHard and Craftsman private labels available for licensing, while Toys 'R' Us' name began to appear on a line of pet toys at Petsmart.

This trend has tempered a bit since then. The bulk of retail brand licensing currently centers on products that are sold in the retailer's own stores (e.g. Hollister collaborating with Keds on flip-flops sold in its stores and on its ecommerce site) or involves the IP of defunct retailers (Wild Oats, Bombay Company).

Still, the idea that a retail brand name can appear in another retail environment to the advantage of both partners remains, as shown by the examples in Exhibit 10.

The current dominant trend focuses on a shop-in-shop model—typically joint ventures or strategic partnerships as opposed to licensing deals—but retail-to-retail licensing endures as well. In fact, just at press time, licensing agency Beanstalk announced that it would represent retailer The Limited for brand-extension licensing into apparel and accessories. The products, it said, would be differentiated from the chain's in-store assortment and would be available in complementary retail channels.

8 Artistic Flair

Art licensing as a sector has been one of the most challenging of any for the last several years, characterized by intense competition and fragmentation, a lack of business knowledge and experience on the part of many artists, and steep barriers when it comes to facing off against higher-profile licenses for partners and retail shelf space.

That said, there are some strong growth areas in the art world, particularly when it comes to licensors of other property types looking for artists with whom to collaborate. They believe artists can help them create something fresh, new, and desirable to allow their own licensing programs to stand out from the crowd and potentially bring in some new fans.

Artist Collaborations

As noted throughout this report, the idea of collaboration has become paramount among celebrity, character/entertainment, fashion, and other areas of licensing, and artists have not been left out of the trend. Some are creating their own collaborations with fashion designers or retailers, but more often they are brought in as one component of a partnership driven by other types of properties.

As Exhibit 11 suggests, these alliances can be classified into five major types, with some individual ventures involving elements from more than one. They include:
- Artists being brought in to refresh or reinterpret a property. This is by far the most common of the five, and involves a wide variety of collaborators.

- Cross-licensing programs pairing two properties, one of which is the artist's imagery.

- Artists collaborating with or inspiring fashion labels.

- Artists creating new imagery tied to a property for use in advertising, promotion, or other marketing initiatives.

- The creation of fine art or prints incorporating a licensed property.

Some artists, including Jeff Koons, Damien Hirst, and Shinzi Katoh, are frequent collaborators with consumer products marketers, retailers, and/or other properties.

Like many of the trends outlined in this report, the combination of art and non-art properties is nothing new. Sports artists have served as licensees of athletes, teams, leagues, and events; painters have incorporated corporate imagery such as Coca-Cola logos or John Deere machinery into their work; and artists have created imagery featuring characters (as in Tom Everhart's longtime collaboration with Peanuts).

But innovative partnerships—from Paul Smith reinterpreting Richard Scarry's children's books *Cars and Trucks* and *Things That Go* to glass artist Dale Chihuly pairing with Pendleton Woolen mills for a blanket collection—are popping up more and more frequently.

Product As Canvas

Increasingly, consumer products are viewed as canvases for artwork, much of it licensed. This has always been the case in certain categories, such as bedding, place mats, and plates, t-shirts and backpacks, and other product segments where surface design has long been in demand. Some of the categories that have served this purpose for years have been particularly popular of late, including wall décor, with giant graphics representing an especially vibrant sector.

But the scope of art-ready surfaces has expanded beyond home furnishings and apparel in recent years. A wide variety of properties, especially characters and artists, are increasingly licensing imagery for products such as surfboards and skateboards, flip-flops, tablet and smartphone cases, artisan candy wrappers, PopTarts and pizza, and appliances, among other examples.

Exhibit 11

Selected Licensing-Related Ventures with Artist Involvement

Type of Initiative	Examples
Artist brought in to refresh or reinterpret a property (often character/entertainment) for a specific collection.	Pepsi's Live for Now collection brought in six street artists to create new imagery tied to Pepsi and soccer for a limited collection; graphic designer Shinzi Katoh creates artwork featuring various licensed characters (Disney, Popeye, Paddington) in his own style for product collections; Romero Britto designed a Barbie doll in his style; Frank Gehry and Cindy Sherman created bags for Louis Vuitton; Lauren Moshi reinterpreted Grateful Dead imagery for line of products; Wayne Hemingway and Jon Burgerman reinterpreted The Beano artwork for specific style guides; Juan Ortiz created imagery of each episode of Star Trek original series in nostalgic poster style, which was then used by licensees; variety of artists created lithos tied to The Big Bang Theory, which were exhibited and featured on limited products; Swimmy Design Lab reinterpreted Ultraman in HOZONHOZON style for a collection of t-shirts and mini-towels.
Artist inspires a fashion label's collection.	Pamela Roland was inspired by T.J. Wilcox's images of the New York skyline; sign painter Josh Luke collaborated with Korean designer JuunJ on a collection.
Artist and non-art property partner for a cross-licensing or collaborative program pairing imagery from the two.	Damien Hirst creates limited scarf edition for Alexander McQueen featuring his Entomology imagery and McQueen's skull motif; Hello Kitty was integrated into Designers Guild archival art for new line of products and into Bea Szenfeld's patterns for use on licensed merchandise.
Use of artist imagery or property reinterpretation for advertising or promotion, sometimes with limited products available.	Disney XD on-air promotions were created by range of artists known for different styles (street artist, animator, poster artist, etc.); Jeff Koons artwork surrounded H&M store to promote museum exhibit, with limited-edition balloon dog purses sold; Mister Cartoon designed bottles for skateboarder Paul Rodriguez' partnership with AXE; Disney promoted Big Hero 6 in Japan with hand-drawn trailers by artist Tekken.
Creation of fine art or art prints featuring a property.	Ant Lucia created Original DC Comics Bombshells art prints, reinterpeting several characters in pin-up style; Costco and Harvest Fine Art launched a sports art program encompassing a 300-print edition of an image featuring NBA players Larry Bird and Magic Johnson, created by artist Stephen Holland and signed by the players and the artist; Mr. Bubble licensed art studio Drizzle Studios for a line of pop-art originals and prints; Tom Zotos created 3D poster art featuring Jimi Hendrix to benefit charity.

Note: Some overlap occurs among sectors.

Source: Raugust Communications

Three key factors are behind this development. First, artists, entertainment licensors, corporate brands with a distinctive look, and other IP owners are looking for new categories to mine. Second, consumer products of all types increasingly feature distinctive colors, designs, or pop culture references as design elements. And third, technology makes it possible for more and more surfaces to become canvases for licensed imagery. As consumers look to personalize their purchases, this trend should continue.

Meanwhile, colors and patterns are becoming more important as brand attributes for licensing. Corporate properties such as Pantone and Fiesta have been expanding their licensing programs, which are based wholly or primarily on their color palettes. And properties from Crayola to Martha Stewart have licensed specific items—in these cases, jewelry and 3D printing filament, respectively—based on colors for which they are known.

Licensing deals tied to brands and properties associated with brightly or uniquely colored patterns, which allow licensees to differentiate their products from others in their category, also are on the rise. The Victoria & Albert Museum, Liberty Fabrics, Loudmouth Golf, French Bull, and a variety of tattoo artists are among the properties that base much of their licensing activity on their distinctive patterns.

Trends in Art Licensing

Some other art-related trends in licensing bear watching:

- Companies that have traditionally served as licensees are starting to license their in-house designs to other manufacturers. T-shirt licensee Junk Food is one example.

- Retailers are increasingly looking to artists for direct-to-retail and retail-exclusive deals. Claire's Stores forged a global DTR deal for 50 products under the Studio Pets by Myrna brand, by photographer Myrna Huijing.

- Artists from around the world are more often expanding their licensing programs across borders. Mandrioli from Italy and GP Deva from Taiwan are two art brands that launched into the U.S. market in 2014.

Art licensing is likely to remain as competitive and challenging as ever, but these and other trends will continue to be bright spots for artists who choose to capitalize on them.

9

Changing Nature of Celebrity

Year after year for close to a decade, many in the licensing community have posited that the celebrity licensing sector was oversaturated and on the verge of decline.

But that hasn't happened yet and is unlikely to do so. More and more celebrity licensing deals—often featuring stars that appeal to increasingly niche target audiences—continuing to be forged on a daily basis, with no end in sight.

Celebrity Is Here To Stay

Not all celebrity programs succeed, of course. But a number of factors suggest that celebrity licensing will remain a strong source of licensed properties for the foreseeable future.

First, celebrities have an increasing number of outlets at their disposal to raise awareness and maintain fan loyalty. These range from a plethora of reality TV opportunities to a growing number of influential print, television, and digital gossip venues.

The nature of today's licensing business, with its focus on short-term collaborations and limited editions, makes it less risky to tie in with a celebrity than in the past. In fact, celebrities' high (albeit sometimes short-lived) profile makes them the ideal focus for such ventures. Their sometimes niche followings also can be a benefit, since they offer something exclusive and desirable to a key, albeit small, consumer group. Celebrities also provide bricks-and-mortar retailers and home shopping venues such as QVC and HSN with the kind of "retailtainment" experience they often seek.

Meanwhile, many celebrities have careers or interests beyond whatever it is that gave them their celebrity. For example, many actresses and actors are interested in design, decorating, crafting, or fitness—all of which lend themselves to logical product extensions—and they want to cultivate that side of their personas. They also are aware that their careers as famous people can be short lived and that licensing or other forms of merchandise extension can offer revenue potential after their initial fame starts to wane.

Finally, unlike in the past, celebrities' penchant for controversy is not a deal-breaker to potential partners any more. While some celebrities' bad behavior has a negative impact on their career in consumer products (e.g., Tiger Woods or Paula Deen), that has become the exception rather than the rule. Most celebrities are able to outlive any controversy that follows them (as has been the case with Martha Stewart and others) and, in some cases (e.g., some Duck Dynasty cast members), their controversial behavior can be part of what makes them appeal to certain consumer groups.

Of course, while celebrity licensing certainly remains strong, the sheer number of properties vying with each other for shelf space and share of mind will mean there will be failures as well as successes.

Dawn of New Celebrity Sectors

The nature and configuration of the celebrity licensing landscape is continually evolving. Exhibit 12 shows 10 major classifications of celebrity licensing, almost all of which are growing quickly in terms of the number of players, for different reasons and in different ways:

- Some have gone from virtually zero as little as five years ago to diverse land-scapes with several successful licensing efforts. Examples include digital-origin celebrities, celebrities that historically worked behind the scenes to support other celebrities (costume designers, stylists, hair and makeup artists), and TV spokespeople.

- Some are well-established but continue to expand as reality television and social media drive awareness. Examples include chefs, interior designers, lifestyle gurus, and models.

- Some have long been popular, but are changing. Examples include athletes, actors, and especially musicians, whose licensing activity increasingly reflects their lives off the field, screen, or stage.

Celebrity product extensions are so common and celebrities are interested in so many areas of business outside of the talent that made them famous that it is increasingly difficult to place a celebrity in one of these major classifications.

Musicians such as Gwen Stefani, Will.i.am, and Pharrell Williams are known almost as much for their fashion design and/or entrepreneurial activities as their music; "pure reality" celebrities such as Paris Hilton and the Kardashians market themselves as designers and businesswomen; and many celebrities are what *Variety* would term "multihyphenates," with their fingers in many different pies. Dannii Minogue, an Australian celebrity who has a fashion collection with the department store Target in that country, describes herself as a singer-songwriter, TV presenter, reality competition host, fashion designer, and actress.

The digital sector, of course, is particularly fast-growing. Digital-origin celebrities may be more influential with certain consumer segments, such as teens or moms of young children, than celebrities associated with traditional media, even though mainstream consumers may be unaware of their existence.

A *Variety* study commissioned in 2014 showed that 10 of the top 20 most influential celebrities among teens, including the top five —Smosh, The Fine Bros., PewDiePie, KSI, and Ryan Hilga—were YouTube stars. Half of the 10 have established licensing programs of some sort at press time.

Meanwhile, the world of celebrity licensing is becoming more and more international, with celebrities from actress Fan Bing Bing in China to Hrithik Roshan in India launching licensed products and brands. Their merchandise is increasingly available beyond the boundaries of their home countries.

Taking the Short View

The bulk of celebrity licensing activity tends to reduce risk by being in the form of capsule collections, limited-edition product lines, or signature lines that are part of a broader promotion.

Exhibit 12

The Blossoming Celebrity Landscape

Sector	Types of Properties	Selected Examples	Typical Licensing Activity
Digital celebrities	YouTube stars; bloggers and vloggers; celebrities from Vine, Twitter, Instagram, Pinterest, Snapchat, "let's play" videos.	Bethany Mota, Aimee Song, Michelle Phan, SMOSH, Sophia Grace and Rosie, Mr. Stampy.	Lifestyle, home, fashion, or beauty products for bloggers and other social media celebrities, usually capsules; novelty products for YouTubers and some social media stars (e.g. comedy).
Behind-the-scenes celebrity and entertainment support	Stylists, make-up artists, costume designers, set designers, hair stylists, magazine editors, and creative directors.	Joe Zee, Cobi Ladner, Cristina Ehrlich, Carolyn Robb, Harold Lancer, Andre Walker, Rachel Zoe, Lori Goldstein, Janie Bryant, Dan Lawson, Jill Ohanneson, Tabitha Coffey.	Products closely related to their expertise: Fashion, cosmetics, hair products, furniture/dé-cor, etc.
Chefs	Bakers and bakery owners, restauran-teurs, TV chefs, cookbook authors, reality foodie-TV hosts, food writers.	Buddy Valastro/Cake Boss, Jane Asher, Curtis Stone, Jamie Oliver, Padma Lakshmi, Ming Tsai, Andrew Zimmern, Fabio Viviani, Dominique Ansel.	Kitchen tools, cook-ware, tableware, and like products. Occa-sionally other home goods and food items.
Models	Victoria's Secret models, plus-size models, mature models, classic/established models.	Kathy Ireland, Iman, Alessandra Ambrosio, Heidi Klum, Carmen Dell'Orefice, Kate Moss.	Lingerie, apparel, accessories, cosmetics, fragrance. Occasionally home goods or other products.
Athletes and fitness gurus (beyond league or players association activities)	Major league athletes with off-field fame and/or style; athletes from individual sports such as swimmers, golfers, cyclists; auto racers; fitness experts.	Shaquille O'Neal, Cam Newton, Jillian Michaels, Jack Nicklaus, David Beckham, Henrik Lundqvist, Arnold Palmer, Bob Greene.	Apparel (often but not always tied to fitness), fitness equipment and accessories, fitness content, supplements, etc. Some go beyond fitness into style-relat-ed categories.
Musicians	Rappers and hip hop artists; country singers; pop stars; music producers and label owners.	Selena Gomez, Britney Spears, Trisha Yearwood, Wiz Khalifa, M.I.A., Nicki Minaj, Snoop Dogg, Carrie Underwood, Keith Urban, Beyon-cé, Jennifer Lopez, Rihanna, Cheryl Cole, Lorde, Rita Ora.	Most are primarily involved in lifestyle apparel, accessories, and fragrance. Some license music-related goods such as earbuds or guitar strings, but the focus is usually broader.

Continued on next page

Continued from last page

Fashion, home, and lifestyle	Fashion designers with personal fame, interior designers, crafting experts, architects.	Jennifer Adams, Nate Berkus, Martha Stewart, Wendy Bellissimo, Bunny Williams, Toby Fairley, Cathy Hobbs, Monica Pederson, Bobby Berk, Paola Navone, Michael Graves, Vern Yip, Genevieve Gorder.	Products related to their expertise, primarily apparel/accessories and home goods.
Actors	Film and television actors and actresses.	Kate Hudson, Hayden Christensen, Zooey Deschanel, Gwyneth Paltrow, Reese Witherspoon, Matthew McConaughey.	Primarily apparel and accessories; occasionally fragrances or home goods.
TV presenters	Reality and competition show hosts, talk show hosts, entertainment show hosts, sports announcers.	Giuliana Rancic, Melissa Rivers, Nick Cannon, Ryan Seacrest, Ellen DeGeneres, Randy Jackson, Tim Gunn, Kirk Herbstreit.	Typically apparel, accessories, and/or home goods.
Pure reality (famous primarily through reality shows) and other celebrity types	Celebrity established primarily through reality shows or other celebrity venue; may subsequently fit into another category.	Kardashians, Paris Hilton, Duck Dynasty castmembers, Jersey Shore castmembers, The Only Way Is Essex castmembers, Bear Grylls, Robb Mariani, Real Housewives castmembers, Donald Trump.	Some are lifestyle-centric and have long-term programs (Paris Hilton), others are multi-category but likely short-term (castmembers of Jersey Shore), and others are focused on expertise (survival and rugged products for Bear Grylls).

Source: Raugust Communications

Traditional licensing deals are not out of the question. Teen social media star Bethany Mota saw her apparel and accessories deal with Aeropostale extended after a year on store shelves, while a number of celebrity chefs have forged long-term licensing deals for cookware, tabletop items, and sometimes foods.

That said, the ability to minimize risk through limited programs gives celebrities opportunities they may not have had otherwise. In fact, stars with ever more niche target markets are coming on the licensing scene every day. Burlesque dancer Dita von Teese, cosplay artist Holly Conrad, florist Thierry Boutemy, *Tank Magazine* CEO and publisher Caroline Issa, and SB.TV founder Jamal Edwards all have licensing or promotional deals in place. Similarly, secondary characters on TV shows are entering licensing. Sadie and Missy Robertson, family members in the Duck Dynasty clan, have signature collections of demure apparel.

The ability to limit risk also gives mainstream celebrities viability that they may not have had in the past and allows them to sign licensing deals in unexpected categories. Examples include Matthew McConnaughey's or Ryan Seacrest's apparel lines, Ellen DeGeneres' lifestyle brand E.D., or Donny Osmond's line of furniture and home décor.

Fragmentation and Evolution

Famous faces, in a seemingly continuous flow, are forging licensing deals, many of them for the first time. But the celebrity sector faces some challenges, especially in traditionally strong areas. With so many different stars coming into the mix, competition is fierce and the market is intensely fragmented.

The fragrance category is emblematic of this landscape. Always an important sector for licensing, the industry has attracted many celebrity licenses over the past decade. In fact, celebrity scents have become as important as the designer fragrances that account for a significant proportion of industry sales. Personalities from Nicki Minaj to Antonio Banderas are among the many that have entered the category.

Scent franchises tied to Britney Spears and Paris Hilton have generated more than $1 billion in sales each, according to several sources. And Elizabeth Taylor's scent franchise, a pioneer in the category, is still going strong.

The first signs that the industry might be oversaturated with licenses occurred in 2014, however, when Elizabeth Arden blamed its lower fourth quarter results on its Justin Bieber and Taylor Swift scents, formerly strong performers whose sales had plummeted sooner than expected. This led to speculation that the crowded celebrity fragrance market in general may finally be experiencing a contraction.

Even in categories beyond fragrance, where celebrity licensing is still on the rise, the nature of the business has changed. Most notably, the bulk of licensing deals are short-lived. Some of the reasons include:

- Strategies that intentionally focus on low-risk capsule collections and other limited ventures, which can be parlayed into longer-term deals or further in-and-out collaborations if successful, but are over quickly if not.

- A high proportion of failures (although since many of the ventures were limited in scope from the beginning, it can be difficult to estimate actual performance).

- Programs that are geared toward very narrow, targeted audiences whose level of demand is satisfied quickly and who tend to move speedily from celebrity to celebrity. This means that even when a short-term program succeeds, the potential for follow-ups is limited.

Despite all of these forces, most licensors' hope is to create a long-term revenue stream, whether through multiple collaborations or by parlaying short-term initial deals into ongoing, traditional licensing initiatives.

Unlike in the past, the focus of celebrity licensing is almost never (except sometimes secondarily) on fan-targeted products. Rather, it is on lifestyle merchandise such as apparel, accessories, beauty products, and home goods that reflect the celebrities' beliefs, image, lifestyle, and/or interests.

Of course, there is room in the market for pure, novelty/collectibles/fan-based celebrity programs, such as those tied to some of the stars of the reality show *Jersey Shore* or the popular tween-targeted band One Direction. There are also one-off opportunities, such as a virtual version of track star Usain Bolt appearing as an in-game-purchase in the mobile app *Temple Run 2*. But these are increasingly the exception rather than the rule.

Celebrities As Creative Directors

Actors, musicians, and other personalities are associating with product manufacturers in a capacity that goes beyond traditional licensing. A frequent occurrence these days is for the celebrity to sign on with a manufacturer as a creative director, overseeing or at least contributing to the development of his or her own signature products, and sometimes other merchandise as well.

Singer Rihanna was named creative director of Puma in December 2014, charged with directing the company's women's line of fitness and training apparel and footwear. The deal is described as a hands-on, multiyear partnership in which Rihanna works with Puma to design new styles and customize classic ones, as well as acting as a global brand ambassador.

New Business Models

Celebrities are increasingly involved with consumer products manufacturers in ways that go beyond licensing, including:

• Financial investments in their product partner's company.

• Input into their partner's overall product development (e.g. as creative director), including but not limited to the signature products.

• A broader brand ambassador relationship in addition to signature products.

• A role as "curator" of collections rather than focusing on products tied to their own name.

Exhibit 13 outlines some examples that illustrate the forms such alternative partnerships can take. Of course, the celebrity's level of actual participation varies. But the trend is for the star to take more control of the development, design, and marketing of their branded products than in the past. Some are as involved in their product ventures as they are in the career that made them famous in the first place.

In addition to partnership ventures such as those shown in the table, a number of celebrities have opted to found their own companies rather than partnering. Reese Witherspoon is launching a lifestyle-products company in 2015; Pharrell Williams introduced a clothing line called ICECREAM, which has served as a licensee for properties such as Despicable Me 2; Jessica Alba's The Honest Company centers on natural products in the baby, body and bath, health and wellness, and cleaning categories; and Melissa Joan Hart founded King of Hearts, a children's clothing line.

Celebrities also are more often launching their product ventures under brand names other than their own. They are placing more emphasis on creating an ongoing venture in a new category than capitalizing on their fame. This is especially true in fashion, where Gwen Stefani's Harajuku Lovers (and other labels), Justin Timberlake's William Rast, and Kate Hudson's Fabletics are a few examples.

Exhibit 13

Selected Celebrity Product Partnerships With Elements Beyond Licensing

Celebrity	Type of Celebrity	Partner	Type of Deal	Category
Cameron Diaz	Actress	Pour la Victoire	Financial investment, artistic director	Footwear, accessories
Carmelo Anthony	NBA player	SMS Audio(1)	Financial investment, endorser	Wearable fitness
Snoop Dogg	Rapper	Sanctiond	Equity partner, limited-edition products	Car care
Katie Holmes (2)	Actress	Alterna	Spokesperson, co-owner, input on product development, potential limited-edition products	Hair care
Katy Perry	Singer	Pop Chips	Financial investment, creative partner, signature flavor	Snacks
Will.i.am (3)	Singer	Coca-Cola/ Ecocycle	Creator of brand, business partner with Coca-Cola	Recycled products
Ashton Kutscher	Actor	Lenovo	Product engineer, spokesperson	Tablets

Continued on next page

Continued from last page

Derek Jeter	Former MLB player	Simon & Schuster	Head of imprint, approval over book signings, input on titles and design	Books
Kathie Lee Gifford	TV presenter	KLG Winery	Joint venture, signature products	Wine
Hallie Berry	Actress	Scandale	Joint venture	Lingerie
David Beckham	Soccer Player	Global Brands Group	Joint venture	Multiple categories of apparel, likely under own name and name of other celebrities
Flo Rida	Rapper	Digital Shelf Space	15% ownership share of operating company, licensing agreement	Exercise videos and other fitness products
Drew Berrymore	Actress	Maesa Group	Co-owner	Fragrances

Notes: (1) Owned by rapper 50 Cent. (2) Holmes was formerly an owner of fashion brand Holmes & Yang.
(3) Will.i.am also is a partner in memBrain Licensing, founding shareholder of Beats Electronics, founder and creator of i.am+ cameras, and director of creative innovation at Intel.
Source: Raugust Communications

10 Beyond Licensing: Changing Business Models

Many of the current trends in licensing, at their core, have to do with a new reliance on alternative business models that either replace or work in concert with traditional licensing. This phenomenon has been particularly noticeable in the celebrity sector, as noted in Chapter 9, but affects many other property types as well.

Promotion and Licensing: Blurred Lines

A significant amount of merchandise tied to licensable properties these days—most notably those tied to celebrities, but also magazines, artists, characters, and a wide variety of other property types—skews more toward the promotional end of the spectrum than the traditional licensing end.

Exhibit 14

Examples of Promotional Deals That Include Signature Product Lines

Property	Partner	Description of Promotion	Products Included
Jeff Koons	H&M	Sponsorship of Museum of Modern Art exhibit, external décor of New York flagship.	Limited-edition line of balloon dog purses at select H&M stores.
Natalie Coughlin	O'Neill 365	Swimmer serves as brand ambassador.	Signature line of apparel.
Ashley Smith	RVCA	Model serves as endorser for the swim and surf brand.	Six capsule collections of signature apparel.
Kid Rock	Harley-Davidson	Sponsorship of musician's Rebel Soul tour, branded experiences at tour stops.	Co-branded Rebel Soul merchandise.
Avengers	Nabisco	In-store promotions, themed packaging across a number of brands.	Cheese Nips imprinted with logos of Avengers characters.
Manchester United	Nike	Wide-ranging sponsorship agreement, official uniform/kit.	Retail apparel and other products, including sub-licensing rights.
Major League Baseball	Church & Dwight	Arm & Hammer and Oxi-Clean are official laundry detergent and stain removers, respectively, of MLB.	Licensed oral care products.
Fifth Harmony	Mattel	Brand ambassadors for Barbie, including creation of brand anthem, appearances, and content.	Doll line featuring the singers.
Disney	Pinnacle Brands	Multiplatform sponsorship deal including live events and other components.	Characters on frozen vegetable packaging.

Continued on next page

Continued from last page

NFL/ San Francisco 49ers	Levi's	Naming rights on stadium.	Levi's x '49ers Collection of jackets, available at stadium, Levi's, and team stores in San Francisco, levi.com.
NBA	Harman	Integrated global partnership as official headphone, speaker, and audio partner, including marketing rights, team deals, on-site activations.	NBA- and player-branded headphones and portable speakers under JBL brand.
Biggest Loser	House	Product placement for Tofu Shirataki noodles to be featured on the show and recipes on the show's website.	Biggest Loser logo on product packaging.
Discovery's Shark Week	Cold Stone Creamery	Sponsorship/marketing deal for weeklong programming event.	Limited-edition Shark Week Frenzy Creation and Great Blue Cupcake ice cream cupcakes.

Source: Raugust Communications

Some product lines, for example, represent one element of a greater promotional or endorsement deal. This tactic has long been used in the sports business, where a sporting goods or apparel company will sign an athlete to endorse its brands, with a signature product line being part of the mix. But the blurring is extending into other sectors of licensing as well.

Exhibit 14 features a handful of examples to illustrate the diversity of promotional deals incorporating licensed merchandise. Property types vary from athletes and sports teams, to fashion designers and models, to musicians and artists, to characters and toys. And disparate partners, including apparel companies, vehicle brands, food and beverage marketers, automotive and household cleaning brands, and retailers are all represented on this small list. The promotional elements and nature of the signature products encompass a range of possibilities as well.

The pool of properties, partners, and products involved in such hybrid promotional-licensing deals promises to grow and become more diverse going forward. Many agents stress as they add new properties to their roster (especially celebrities but also other types) that they are handling endorsement and promotional opportunities as well as branding and licensing.

It should be noted that technology advancements—as with so many other areas of licensing—have helped spur this trend. Print-on-demand platforms, the ability to print on diverse surfaces (such as foods), and other innovations have made it possible to create short runs of products faster and more economically than in the past, allowing for the quick and cost-effective turnaround of unique products within the umbrella of a promotional deal.

Capsule collections and limited editions, which are so ubiquitous in the licensing business these days (and are discussed in more detail in Chapter 12), also contribute to the blending of promotion and licensing. While they generate royalty income (as do product lines as part of endorsements or promotions in most cases), much of the impetus behind them is to create a promotional splash.

Curation and Inspiration

Curation is another growing technique that crosses into the realms of both promotion and licensing. Curation involves a collection of existing merchandise that is inspired by a particular property and assembled by someone tied to that property. While there may be a licensed or branded component, that is not the core of the collection.

As Exhibit 15 illustrates, most of the properties involved in curation to date have been in the realms of celebrity, entertainment (especially TV and film), and magazine brands, leaving room for diversification. Partners for curated collections have skewed toward home shopping networks and subscription/membership ecommerce sites, but traditional retailers such as Gap and Target are increasingly testing the waters. HSN and Cost Plus World Markets were two of the earliest adopters of this technique and continue to be among the most active.

Exhibit 15

Examples of Curated Product Lines Tied to Licensed Properties

Property	Licensor	Partner	Description	Original Licensed Products Involved?
White Collar	USA Network	Gilt.com	Matt Bohmer-curated collection of men's accessories inspired by the actor's character on the show.	Bohmer-designed pocket square as giveaway.
The Notebook, The Longest Ride, and Dear John	Nicholas Sparks	Joss & Main	Curated collection of home goods inspired by the three Sparks novels.	No.
Andrew Zimmern	Andrew Zimmern	Quarterly Co.	Gift boxes of handpicked items the chef finds inspiring, delivered every three months to subscribers.	No.

Continued on next page

Continued from last page

Rachel Zoe	Rachel Zoe	ShoeDazzle	Monthly curated collections by celebrity stylist Zoe, serving as "chief stylist" for the site.	No.
GQ	Conde Nast	Gap	Curated collection of items designed by Best New Menswear Designers named by the magazine.	Designers contributed original products for the venture.
Univision	Univision	HSN	Boutique Univision for products that appeal to Hispanics, from a variety of HSN partner brands and designers.	No original products, but many of the curated brands are licensed, with properties including Wolfgang Puck, Coca-Cola, G. by Giuliana, and Vince Camuto.
Malificent, Cinderella, The Hundred Foot Journey	Disney	HSN	Curated collection of products from HSN designers and brands that reflect the design and ambiance of the films.	No, but previous similar deal with Disney's Oz the Great and Powerful included licensed as well as curated products.
Elle	Hearst	Net-a-Porter	Curated selection of beauty products including hair, nail, and skin care, as well as makeup and fragrance.	No.
Wired	Conde Nast	Target	Assortment of tech gadgets from vendors such as NuForce and Adonit, ranging from earbuds to camera lenses, curated by Wired editors, displayed in a Wired-branded endcap.	No, but partners stated at the outset that the addition of Wired licensed products was possible in the future.
Eat Pray Love	Sony	Cost Plus World Market	Curated selection of products inspired by the three countries featured in the film.	A few EPL-branded products were in the mix.

Source: Raugust Communications

The term curation has become a bit of a buzzword in the licensing, consumer products, and retailing sectors, and sometimes has a different definition than the one we are using here. For example, celebrity-based licensing programs occasionally are represented as being "curated" by the celebrity, even though the merchandise is licensed in the traditional sense.

For example, Macy's Ryan Seacrest Distinction brand is described as curated by Seacrest; licensees include PVH, Peerless, and Randa Accessories. In cases such as these, the term often suggests that the design direction is coming more from the licensees or retailer than the celebrity.

Focus on "Partnership"

Licensors and licensees are increasingly crossing beyond traditional licensing agreements into the realms of strategic alliances, strategic partnerships, and joint ventures. In some cases, these terms are just a matter of semantics. The partners often are simply using them to describe a traditional licensing agreement in an attempt to highlight the importance of the deal to both parties.

In a growing number of instances, however, the alliance between the property owner and the manufacturer, retailer, or service provider does qualify as something other than licensing. Some of the situations that lend themselves to such alternative business structures include:

- Technological enhancements. Jakks Pacific and Nantworks have a joint venture to create interactive toys in a partnership with Disney, which has exclusive rights (along with some Jakks properties) to the technology in the category.

- International distribution. PVH has a joint venture with Gazal for its PVH Brands business in Australia, which includes the Calvin Klein, Tommy Hilfiger, Van Heusen, and other fashion labels.

- Property acquisition. Iconix Brand Group purchased 51% of the Buffalo David Bitton brand by forming a new joint venture with Buffalo International ULC (the brand's former owner). Iconix controls the brand and Buffalo International remains as the core licensee.

- Property development and distribution. POW Entertainment, Genius Brands, and Archie Comics launched a joint venture to oversee the comic and film property, Stan Lee's Mighty 7, while Cartoon Network and LEGO Group jointly created the Mixels brand, which includes animation, digital gaming, collectible building toys, and licensed merchandise.

- E-commerce and retail. Genesis Luxury Fashion has partnerships with licensed brands including Burberry and BottegaVeneta to distribute their labels in India, through both branded retail stores and wholesale channels.

Beyond these common scenarios, companies sometimes opt for joint ventures or strategic alliances even in situations that normally are accomplished through traditional licensing deals. When Chicken Soup for the Soul launched its line of comfort foods, it did so through a joint venture with Daymon Worldwide Global Brands, a branding and sourcing company. And Paws describes its alliance with Card.com for Garfield prepaid debit cards as a strategic partnership.

In many of these cases, the key factor in doing some sort of joint venture or strategic alliance in lieu of a traditional licensing deal is to share the risk and investment and compel both partners to put their all into making the initiative a success.

Continuing Rise of Investment Groups

The Great Recession of 2007-2008 helped prompt the rise of investment companies buying moribund or struggling brands and attempting to reverse their fortunes. They have often relied on 100% licensing strategies to do so. Some of these companies tend to sell off the brands once they are on a path toward success, in a typical venture capital model, while others continue to manage the brands on an ongoing basis. The corporate, fashion, and "lifestyle" sectors have been affected the most by this trend.

Another area where investment groups are playing an expanding role is among properties that need to ensure their future existence. The latter category includes many celebrity brands; in recent years, Authentic Brands Group purchased the Elvis Presley, Marilyn Monroe, and Muhammad Ali estates, while Iconix acquired an 80% share in Charles Schulz's Peanuts business.

This strategy could become more commonplace in the coming years as some creator-controlled character properties, especially those with ongoing lifestyle-product opportunities, look for ways to extend their legacies as their creators look toward retirement.

Exhibit 16 summarizes the portfolio holdings of some of the key players in licensed property investment.

Property acquisitions are not limited just to investment specialists, of course. FAM Brands, an owner of fashion labels as well as an apparel licensee, purchased the Bally Total Fitness brand (of which it had been the master licensee for clothing) in 2013, among other recent acquisitions, and is licensing it out into other categories.

Alternatives For Agencies

There are few participants in the licensing business that have been facing more changes in how they do business than licensing agencies, which are operating in a more crowded market than ever before. Not only are they dealing with the same issues as all licensing companies, but they are seeing more competition as licensing executives continue to be downsized and often end up starting their own independent firms.

Exhibit 16

Selected Investment Companies Specializing in Licensed Properties and a 100% Licensing Model

Company	Selected Properties in Portfolio (1)	Selected Recent Deals
Iconix Brand Group	Candie's, Badgley Mischka, Joe Boxer, Mossimo, London Fog, Op, Danskin, Peanuts, Ed Hardy, Marc Ecko, Material Girl, Umbro, Cannon, Field-crest, Waverly, Sandra by Sandra Lee, Sharper Image, Starter.	Purchased PONY (2015), Strawberry Shortcake (2015), Airwalk and other Collective Licensing brands (2014), Buffalo David Bitton (2013), Juicy Couture (2013), Spyder (2013).
Authentic Brands Group	Elvis Presley, Muhammad Ali, Marilyn Monroe, Juicy Couture, Judith Lieber, Adrienne Vittadini, Taryn Rose, Spyder, Prince.	Purchased Elvis Presley (2013), Muhammad Ali (2013).
Sequential Brands	William Rast, Ellen Tracy, Avia, And1, Revo, Heelys, People's Liberation, Caribbean Joe, Linens & Things, Franklin Mint.	Purchased Galaxy Brands Group including And1 and Avia brands (2014), Franklin Mint (2013).
Hilco Brands	Polaroid, Halston, Portico, Under the Canopy (some are co-owned with Gordon Brothers and others).	Purchased Portico and Under the Canopy (2013); sold Linens 'n Things (2013).
Xcel Brands	Isaac Mizrahi, Judith Ripka, Liz Claiborne NY.	Purchased Judith Ripka (2014).

Notes: (1) Wholly or partially owned.
Source: Raugust Communications

Meanwhile, more service companies outside of the business are launching licensing divisions. PR and communications firms such as miPR and Peppercom, branding and marketing agencies including Brandemonium and Rizon Studios, talent agencies such as United Talent Agency (UTA) and William Morris Endeavour (WME), and ad agencies such as Omnicom (a pioneer in this trend with its purchase of Beanstalk in the mid-2000s), are among the examples of non-licensing companies adding licensing agency arms through launches or acquisitions over the last decade.

To address these competitive forces, licensing agencies are taking a number of steps to diversify their business models:

- Adding services, such as consulting, PR, digital content production and distribution, style guide design, and training. The last is particularly true for art-licensing specialists.

- Brokering one-off deals, as well as representing licensors on a continuing basis.

- Specializing in specific categories such as food, digital content, or publishing, where deep expertise sets them apart, or signing to represent clients for single categories.

- Serving both licensors and licensees, representing the former for outbound and the latter for inbound licensing.

- Representing properties for so-called 360° deals, which extend further than licensing into management, appearances, and so on. The music licensing business is one area where this trend has taken hold.

- Adding new payment structures aside from traditional commissions, such as retainers, fees for specific services, or percentages of sales.

- Forging alliances with other agents to mutually add geographic reach, new specialties, or more clients.

The last tactic has been particularly frequent of late. Beanstalk and Indian licensing agency Wild East Group formed a strategic partnership for licensing of local properties and Beanstalk's global brands in India, while Synergy Licensing and The Brand Liaison partnered to collaboratively offer a broader range of services.

Consolidation is also a factor, as companies from inside and outside licensing acquire agencies as a means to enter or expand their services in the business. Li & Fung, the global logistics and distribution company that serves as a licensor, licensee, and vendor for direct-to-retail agreements, purchased The Licensing Company, a global licensing agency specializing in corporate and fashion brands, and RM Enterprises, a character licensing agency in Asia, for example.

11

Retail: A Need for New Niches

The retail landscape continues to evolve. As some channels (including mass bricks-and-mortar retail) become more difficult and competitive for licensing, others—many of them emerging or niche—are opening up as opportunities for licensors and licensees.

E-Commerce Evolution

When it comes to licensing potential, e-commerce has evolved well beyond the first wave of players, which consisted of online-only ("pure-play") specialists, such as Amazon in the U.S. or T-Mall in China, and the e-commerce operations of physical retailers ("bricks-and-clicks").

Today, a growing pool of online retailers are involved in licensing, including:
- Personalization/print-on-demand sites. CaféPress offers licensed products tied to properties from Mr. Bean to Hunger Games.

- Aggregators. ShoeDazzle has collaborated with celebrities such as stylist Rachel Zoe (for a curated collection), while Zappos.com paired its The Cool People private label with celebrity Melissa Rivers.

- Flash sale and membership sites. Birchbox has worked with USA Network on a collection tied to its series *Suits*; JustFab Inc. works with Kate Hudson on her Fabletics line of lifestyle/athletic apparel and accessories; Joss & Main has created a curated collection of 150 existing home décor products inspired by Fox's *Home Alone*.

Of course, the pure-play and bricks-and-clicks segments are still going strong as well, and new trends never cease to unfold. On the pure play side, for example, the landscape of concepts continues to expand:
- ReedPOP, which organizes comic and fan conventions, operates an online store for convention exclusives and unique licensed merchandise, many in limited editions.

- Ship and Duck is an online space that pairs manufacturers with licensors to develop unique limited-edition products, such as handmade wooden iPhone cases under the Chris-Craft boat brand.

- Amazon has worked with licensors on merchandise boutiques, including with Nickelodeon for holiday shops featuring more than 100 price-discounted products across a variety of properties and categories.

- Spotify paired with BandPage to allow music artists who are streamed on the site to offer merchandise, experiences, and tickets to fans.

Meanwhile, sites ranging from luxury e-tailers Net-A-Porter and eLuxe to home furnishings e-shop Ballard Designs to apparel site MyTheresa.com are entering into licensed collaborations with celebrities, fashion labels, and other properties.

Globally, e-commerce has become the key for global brands to enter some new markets, notably China. Brand marketers such as Westinghouse and retailers such as TopShop are increasingly embarking on an e-commerce-only strategy to enter the territory, although they may expand into bricks-and-mortar retail later.

The Emergence of Social Commerce

As consumers move away from laptops and traditional websites to mobile devices and social networking, more opportunities are emerging for licensing in those avenues. As of late 2014, retailers such as Target are experimenting with encouraging consumers to compare prices via mobile app while they are in the store, while social sites such as Facebook, Twitter, and Google are testing ways to seamlessly allow users to buy products they see on social platforms.

Social Shopping

Social networking and e-shopping are increasingly merging, offering a new venue for the sale and viral promotion of licensed merchandise.

Sophie Simmons, a model and designer (and reality star, thanks to her appearances on her father's show, *Gene Simmons: Family Jewels*), has been the focus of one early deal in this space. She created a capsule collection in fall 2014 for The Style Club, billed as "a seamless fusion of ecommerce shop, video channel, and social platform."

That led to her creating another collection for New Year's Eve, as well as joining the company as brand ambassador and creative consultant, where she will help guide the design of clothing for women of all sizes.

Other early examples of licensing within the social shopping sphere:

• IKEA experimented with selling merchandise through Instagram in a promotion in Russia.

• Apparel company Roots offered men's and women's tops and accessories in collaboration with artist Douglas Coupland through a pop-up shop on Twitter.

• NFL Players Inc. partnered with social commerce platform Stylinity to allow users to view selfies of NFL players wearing their favorite styles, click on items they like, and be transferred to the licensee's e-commerce website.

As with e-commerce, social commerce has been particularly important for licensing in less-developed territories, such as China. That country has seen consumers start to transition to social commerce through stores on the texting platform WeChat and through the mobile shopping app Koudi.

Importance of Home Shopping

Home shopping has become a key means of launching new properties. Home shopping networks also serve as the home for ongoing DTR or exclusive licensing programs in many cases.

Fashion labels and celebrities have a particularly high profile on this platform. But companies such as QVC and HSN also work with properties from other realms, notably corporate and entertainment licensing, as long as they lend themselves to the apparel, accessories, beauty, home, and lifestyle categories in which the channels specialize. Ellen DeGeneres' new E.D. line includes an exclusive collection called E.D. On Air with QVC, while Fremantle Media's Deadliest Catch partnered with ShopHQ for a show featuring seafood and other licensed food and kitchen items.

These venues can sell a lot of merchandise, but much of their value comes from their ability to create awareness for a property and add an "experiential" twist. Lengthy on-air appearances by the celebrities, designers, or executives associated with a property (e.g., a magazine's editor) enable viewers to get to know the products and creators and the story behind them, and to be educated and entertained. And appearances are well-promoted on-air.

A number of ventures in 2014 experimented with making the home shopping experience more immediate and creating a closer connection between content and product purchase. Target partnered with TBS for product placement of its Nate Berkus product line within an episode of *Cougar Town*; consumers could click on the products on their smartphones or tablets during an online simulcast and purchase goods in real time at Target.com. And H&M allowed fans watching the 2014 Super Bowl on Samsung smart televisions to purchase David Beckham bodywear by using their remote during a 30-second Super Bowl spot.

Licensors have long been seeking ways to more closely connect fans' entertainment viewing and their product purchasing, and these types of ventures, along with the emergence of social shopping, are another step toward the day when that possibility may become a reality for mainstream consumers.

Bricks-and-Mortar: Niche Opportunities Continue to Expand

Most of the highly publicized new venues for licensed merchandise are in the digital sphere, as discussed above. Meanwhile, most of the talk about bricks-and-mortar retail focuses on the challenges, such as declining shelf space, more competition among properties, and consolidation among a relatively few licensors. All of these are real and ongoing.

There are some growth areas within the traditional retail sphere, however. They may be niche opportunities in many cases, but they offer established properties the potential for incremental revenue-generation, as well as opportunities for new properties if they are a good fit.

Some areas of interest include:
- Channels that have opened up due to changing perceptions. Just as value and off-price retailers have gone from taboo to desirable in the past five or more years, outlet stores are emerging as acceptable venues for licensed goods. Properties including (RED), Oscar de la Renta, Snoop Dogg, and Alexander McQueen have partnered with bricks-and-mortar outlet malls such as Europe's Chic Outlet Shopping and online sites such as Outnet and Overstock.com.

- Retailers that have traditionally focused on private labels or national brands (and sometimes licensed goods) but have become new players in direct-to-retail licensing. Plus-size retailers Lane Bryant and Swimsuits for all have worked with Isabel Toledo and blogger Gabi Gregg, respectively, while Carphone Warehouse and Best Buy have forged deals for fashionable electronics accessories, the first with Kate Moss and the second with Kate Spade New York.

- Shops associated with entertainment venues and other nontraditional locations that are forging partnerships with licensed properties. The New York Botanical Garden has partnered with Oscar de la Renta for a line of 20 tabletop items and the luxury condo-hotel development Costa Hollywood with the fashion label Indie Soul.

As these examples show, despite the seeming saturation of licensing at retail, there continue to be new channels that are ripe for cultivation, at least for properties that make sense.

Global Deals

The idea of direct-to-retail and retail-exclusive licensing deals that span the globe have long been a hope but never a reality. Varying tastes from country to country, global retailers' uneven strengths and weaknesses in individual regions, and retail chains' localized buying practices are among the factors making global retail deals a challenge.

But the landscape has started to change somewhat, particularly in the specialty apparel sector. Since fall 2013, a growing number of fast-fashion retailers (and other fashion-based retailers) have been signing deals that are termed as global, meaning that they extend across most if not all of the retailer's outlets across the world, at least in all the territories where they are present.

Examples include:
- Uniqlo, headquartered in Japan. It has signed partnerships with properties such

as Moomin and Popeye to be distributed throughout its 1,200 stores in 14 markets.

- Topshop, based in the U.K. It paired with Kate Moss for a design collaboration sold in its stores in 40 countries and online, as well as in pop-up shops in department stores in territories where it is not located.

- Pull & Bear, headquartered in Spain. It signed a deal to create a line of Goodyear vintage t-shirts and sweatshirts in its stores in 62 countries, and online.

- Claire's, based in the U.S. It launched a Katy Perry Prism line of jewelry and accessories in more than 3,000 of its stores in 44 countries, including 1,500 in the U.S.

None of these retailers is global in the sense of being present or equally strong in every territory (there are 196 countries in the world) but many of them operate in most of the key territories for licensing (and beyond). As the Internet and social media make fashion and tastes a bit more global and create worldwide awareness for properties, no matter where they come from, this trend is likely to strengthen.

Still, in retail channels outside of specialty fashion, buying continues to occur on a country-by-country basis, which makes forging a global deal difficult. And, even as tastes are becoming somewhat more similar worldwide, there are still numerous differences from country to country, especially in terms of product specifications (colors, sizes, styles, etc.). These and other factors make worldwide deals impractical.

Multiple Exclusivity

Offering something exclusive to each retailer remains a necessity. Whether an exclusive capsule collection or a direct-to-retail deal, exclusive deals between licensors and/or licensees and retailers remain a key strategy. That said, retail exclusives involving established properties increasingly tend to be narrow and to coexist with other, ostensibly non-competitive exclusives.

When retail fashion collaborations first came on the scene, they typically were solo affairs involving one property (frequently a character, brand, celebrity, or designer) and a single retailer. The success of such ventures led established properties to forge ongoing series of collaborations with various retailers, one after the other. As of late 2014, the trend for many larger licensors, especially in the character and corporate sectors, is to release multiple collaborations with retailers and designer boutiques simultaneously.

This multiple-exclusive strategy occurs in support of an anniversary or film release, but also as a strategy without a link to such an event. The exclusives take several forms:
- Many involve unique retailers in each geographic market. Playboy celebrated its 60th anniversary in 2014 with products from designers including Lucien Pellat Finet, Hillier, Onyva, and others sold exclusively through boutiques including Colette in Paris, Isetan in Tokyo, and ZoZo Villa Lane Crawford in Asia. Iconix relies on direct-to-retail agreements in each market for its fashion labels.

- Some are differentiated by demographic target. Mattel forged apparel partnerships for Barbie with Forever 21, Uniqlo, Primark, Wildfox, and Lord & Taylor, each targeting a different consumer group.

• Some involve exclusive characters or sub-brands, or a few exclusive items. Nickelodeon and licensee Playmates Toys granted Walmart exclusive rights for the launch of action figures tied to two characters, Bebop and Rocksteady, before their debut in the third season of the *Teenage Mutant Ninja Turtles* TV series.

Even power players in the fashion collaboration field are open to having their exclusives narrowed slightly on occasion. When the luxury label Joseph Altuzarra created a capsule collection for Target in 2014, an "edited assortment" of the products also were sold through the luxury etailer Net-A-Porter.com.

Wholesale and Trade Opportunities

As the retail scene becomes more and more crowded with licensed products, some property owners are looking for opportunities to reach consumers through wholesalers or distributors—companies that market to the trade rather than directly to consumers—in addition to their retail offerings.

For example, Condé Nast worked with fine art publisher New Era Portfolio to offer museum-quality images from Conde Nast's library exclusively to design professionals, to be used as part of their interior design projects. And Xcel Brands licensed Isaac Mizrahi New York to Chef's Diet National, a meal-delivery service focusing on fresh gourmet diet programs; the fashion designer created limited-edition co-branded cooler bags used for delivery.

The food service area is another example. Sunny Sky Products manufactures and distributes specialty dispensed beverages to convenience stores and other food service channels, and has licensed Jolly Rancher for its portfolio of flavor mixes. Similarly, J&J Snack foods licensed Oreo for a churro snack that it distributes to quick-service restaurants, sports arenas, and outlets within the food-service channel.

It should be noted that licensed properties' profile within the food service industry in general, both through distributors and directly with food service outlets, is on the rise as well, as Exhibit 17 shows. Bakeries in particular have featured licensed properties in hybrid promotional-licensing deals that feature cookies, cupcakes, and the like with character-based decoration or property-specific flavors.

Programs with distributors and wholesalers create incremental revenue streams for licensors, in a not-yet-crowded space. They can help generate awareness and a track record that can be parlayed into retail product deals, which is important for properties that are not yet heavily licensed. While the technique is emerging only slowly, it is likely to gain traction over time.

Exhibit 17

Selected Use of Licensed Properties in Food Service

Food Service Provider	Licensed Tie-In	Timeframe	Nature of Promotions/Products
Rita's Italian Ice	Starburst	Limited	Special flavors; has done similar tie-ins with Jelly Belly and others
Yogurtland	Looney Tunes	Limited	Special flavors, plus premiums
Sonic	Colleges	Limited	College logos stamped on buns of localized burgers
Biscuiteers (U.K. cookie boutique)	Mr. Men and Little Miss	Limited	Hand-made, hand-iced biscuits (cookies) and cakes in an illustrated box
Dunkin' Donuts	Arnold Palmer	Limited	Special-flavored Coolatta, made with licensee Arizona Beverages' product; Oreo and Minute Maid are other brands available
Sunny Sky Products (manufacturer and distributor of specialty dispensed beverages)	Jolly Rancher	Long-term license	Concentrated and ready -to-use flavor mixes for frozen carbonated and non-carbonated frozen beverages for dispensers
Krispy Kreme	Ghostbusters	Limited	Ghostbusters and Stay Puft Marshmallow doughnuts in U.S. and Canada
J&J Snack Foods	Oreo	Long-term license	Oreo Churros to be sold nationwide through the food service channel including quick service restaurants, convenience stores, sports and leisure venues, etc.

Source: Raugust Communications

12

Dipping a Toe Before Taking a Deep Dive

The challenging global retailing landscape lingers, and many facets of the worldwide economy are still a concern. Consumers' tastes are changing ever more quickly, hastened by social media. And the licensed product scene is becoming continually more crowded. For all of these reasons, a key consideration in any licensing deal is how to minimize risk. That thought process often leads to some sort of test before stepping forward in a bigger way (if warranted).

In fact, many of the trends discussed throughout this report, while they have other benefits, have become established, in part, because they serve as a means of testing new partnerships and incubating new properties. Curation, crowdfunding, pop-up shops, personalization, user-generated content, social media monitoring, the combination of promotional and licensing techniques, fast fashion, and retail exclusives all have an element of testing built in. Capsule collections and limited editions, so ubiquitous these days, also represent, at their core, a chance to test a property or product line.

This is not to say that traditional, long-term licensing deals will go away, of course, but even these increasingly have a testing period built in to the contract.

Limited editions and capsule collections

As is evident throughout this report, capsule collections (which consist of a limited number of products) and limited editions (which involve a limited number of units or a limited time period of availability) are almost becoming the norm. They cross nearly every property type and product category, although much of the activity is centered on apparel and accessories tied to celebrities, entertainment properties, artists, and fashion designers.

Exhibit 18

Selected Examples of Limited Editions and Capsule Collections Involving Licensed Properties

Description of Partnership	Scope of Deal
Summit Entertainment/ Lionsgate with Sephora for the film Divergent	Limited-edition eye shadow, blush, bronzer, lip gloss, and nail polishes in freestanding Sephora stores, online, and in Sephora at JCPenney boutiques
Lucky Brand Jeans with Cone Mills	Capsule collection of made-in-America jeans in which both the denim itself and the cutting and sewing were sourced domestically.
Jay Z with Barneys for a holiday collection	Short-term boutique of limited-edition products created by Jay Z in collaboration with Lanvin, Balenciago, Balmain, Proenza Schouler, Rick Owens, Moncler.
Sports analyst Kirk Herbstreit with John Morrell's Eckrich division	Limited-edition line of smoked sausage available for a limited time at start of college football season, part of a larger promotional deal.
Fred Segal and Lenny Kravitz/ Kravitz Design	10 limited-edition apparel, accessories, travel accessories items and a limited-edition motorcycle sold through Fred Segal stores globally. Items roll out over a 12-month period.
Nicola Formichetti and Didier Dubot Joaillerie	Capsule collection of high-end jewelry available at three stores in Tokyo and New York.
Zooey Deschanel and Tommy Hilfiger	16-piece capsule dress and accessory collection sold at select Tommy Hilfiger and Macy's stores and their respective websites.
Speedo with swimmer Natalie Coughlin and artist Adhemas Batista	Limited-edition line of swim caps under the "Art of the Cap" promotional banner, involving its five athlete-endorsers and five artists, with the focal point being the Coughlin/Batista collaboration. Proceeds go to charity.
Twentieth Century Fox and Hot Topic for movie Book of Life	Limited-edition apparel collection inspired by the Dia de los Muertos-themed film, including dresses, tops, skirts, cardigans, as well as jewelry, accessories, and fragrance.
Spangler Candy and Dr. Pepper Snapple Group	Two limited-edition Hawaiian Punch flavors of Dum Dums within a 16-flavor bag of the candy. Quantities of the limited-edition suckers to total 30 million.

Source: Raugust Communications

The two techniques overlap: Capsule collections are nearly always limited in number of units and time available, as well as number of SKUs, while product lines described as limited editions, in turn, typically involve just a few products.

Exhibit 18 examines a tiny fraction of the recent deals involving capsule collections, limited editions, or both. While by no means comprehensive, it serves to illustrate the diversity of deals. (Note that this trend is closely related to the rise in collaborations discussed in Chapter 7, most of which are limited in nature.)

Many capsules and limited editions also are viewed primarily as promotional ventures—although they do typically generate some sort of royalty per unit—and, as such, are sometimes handled by marketing or promotions staff rather than licensing personnel. That said, if a capsule or limited edition is successful, the possibility always exists for a regular series of short-term collaborations or a transition into a traditional licensing deal. Both developments involve a move toward the sales and revenue-generation end of the spectrum.

In some cases, a capsule or limited edition is meant as a precursor to a longer-term program, right from the beginning. Major League Baseball and the pop culture/art brand Tokidoki, for example, paired for a cross-licensing initiative that launched with a limited product assortment at the beginning of the 2014 baseball season. A plan was in place for a full rollout later in the year. (More than a half dozen MLB licensees were involved.)

A Sip Before a Swallow: Testing the Retail Coffee Market

The food and beverage industry has long been a place where limited market testing typically precedes a new product rollout.

A recent example is Kraft's new line of McCafé packaged coffee, under license from McDonald's, which it is introducing nationally in food retailers in 2015. The coast-to-coast launch follows market tests, as is the norm for multinational consumer products marketers such as Kraft. Licensors and licensees across sectors are increasingly emulating this strategy.

In other cases, a venture is planned as a one-time limited edition or capsule, but expands into a long-term deal due to positive results. In 2013 Kellogg's partnered with Rocky Mountain Chocolate Factory for a limited-edition breakfast cereal, available at selected Target stores. The success of that venture led Kellogg's to roll out the product line for the long term across all of its retail channels.

Limited editions and/or capsule collections also can be part of a broader deal. For example, singer Katy Perry's two-year licensing agreement with Claire's incorporated some in-and-out seasonal pieces, limited-edition items, and "collectibles" as part of the longer-term effort. In this case, testing is not necessarily a key objective.

Capsules and limited editions typically are focused on a single retailer; retail exclusives, discussed in Chapter 11, present another means of testing a property or new initiative, among other objectives.

Of course, licensors and their licensees also use traditional testing mechanisms to gain confidence before launching a line that is intended to last a long time. Licensed foods sold through supermarkets, for example, are introduced in limited test markets before the partners undertake a full launch.

Exhibit 19

Multiproperty Licensing Initiatives From Selected Licensors

Program	Properties	Description of Venture
Disney Villains	Cruella de Vil, Maleficent, Evil Queen, Ursula.	Licensing program with partners including Kiss Products for limited-edition kits at Walgreens.
GQ's Best New Menswear Designers	Four emerging menswear designers who are winners of the magazine's annual competition.	Exclusive menswear collection at The Gap, including approximately 15 categories of men's apparel and accessories in the four signature styles.
DreamWorks' Storytellers Collection	Aggregates characters from Shrek, Madagascar, How to Train Your Dragon, and Kung Fu Panda.	Studio's in-house publishing imprint, DreamWorks Press, publishes books under the banner.
Skylanders Universe (Activision)	Characters and worlds from all the Skylanders franchises.	Licensee Penguin uses the banner for all of its fiction publishing tied to the property, which brings all the franchises into a single unified world.
WB True Classics (Warner Bros.)	Looney Tunes, Hanna-Barbera, and other classic characters.	Multicategory licensing effort in the EMEA region.
Disney and Pixar Animation Studios Artist Showcase	Original properties created by artists, animators, and writers who work at the Disney and Pixar animation studios.	Publishing program through Disney's in-house publishing arm, Disney Worldwide Publishing.
DC Comics Bombshells	Female DC Comics characters including Wonder Woman, Poison Ivy, Supergirl, Catwoman, others.	Licensee Quantum Mechanix line of art prints in nostalgic pin-up style.
UNITED XXVI Collection	Vine stars Nash Grier, Hayes Grier, Cameron Dallas, and Carter Reynolds.	Aeropostale collection including pieces designed by all four, along with the retailer's designers.

Source: Raugust Communications

Licensors with control over a portfolio of properties are increasingly launching multi-property franchises that allow them to maintain a constant footprint at retail. They can offer a consistent presence but with a changing assortment combining high-profile "hot" properties and new introductions.

Meanwhile, they can test the potential of some of the latter to break out while they are riding the coattails of their more successful siblings. If one does particularly well as part of the group, it can then be positioned as a separate property.

As Exhibit 19 illustrates, much of this activity emanates from the entertainment/character sector, with licensors driving the strategy. But there is potential in other arenas, particularly fashion and celebrity, and for programs initiated by licensees or retailers.

Ventures that are representative of this trend take different forms:
- Some are focused on secondary characters (Disney Villains or Warner Bros.' women of DC Comics).

- Some focus on a combination of high-profile and lesser-known properties (WB True Classics, which focuses on main characters across franchises, but offers opportunities for less well-known characters as well).

- Some are a way to bring diverse properties together for storytelling purposes (Skylanders Universe or the Dreamworks Storytellers Collection).

- Some encompass entirely new or emerging properties (GQ's Best New Menswear Designers, Disney/Pixar's publishing program for its artists' original properties, Aeropostale's gathering of four Vine stars under one brand).

Not all licensors have a broad enough portfolio of properties to emulate this trend on their own, of course. But, with licensing executives so willing to consider various sorts of partnerships, and with licensees and retailers in a position to assist in such alliances, the appearance on retail shelves of initiatives focusing on groups of characters could continue to grow.

Staying On the Shallow End

While ventures such as those discussed in this chapter offer a certain cachet to the right brands and generate awareness through their perceived uniqueness and rarity, testing is certainly part of the mix of objectives in many cases.

Some property owners, however, do not necessarily have designs on a long-term, traditional licensing strategy. They may prefer to follow a consistent strategy of sequential or simultaneous capsules and limited editions that do not transition to long-term programs, even if the short-term ventures dictate that the latter is viable.

Fashion labels in the streetwear sector have a brand positioning that is predicated on them not being perceived as mainstream; opting for series of short-term collaborations and collections keeps them desirable and interesting to their core fans.

Similarly, for the big movie studios and other well-established classic properties, putting together a continual series of higher-end, fashion-driven, short-term ventures—especially in conjunction with key events such as anniversaries or new releases—generates awareness, keeps higher-end consumers in the loop, and lends a trend-forward halo to the property. This is true even when a standard mass-directed licensing effort continues in parallel.

Retailers with fast-fashion strategies also are typically looking more for short-term interest and other inherent benefits, rather than the potential for longer relationships. In some instances longer-term alliances may come out of a successful series of limited ventures, but that is not often the goal upfront.

13 Branding Boost

The terms *brands* and *branding*, with their wide spectrum of definitions, have become important across nearly all property types and product categories, in a growing number of territories, and in a variety of permutations.

In some ways, this trend serves as a counterbalance to the other developments outlined in this book, many of which stress short-term or limited initiatives.

Global Embrace of Corporate Licensing

Corporate brand-extension licensing has long been established and vibrant in the U.S. and Canada, although it began leveling off in the mid-2010s due to competition and other issues. A newer phenomenon is the growth of corporate brand-extension licensing outside of the U.S. and Canada. Certain mature licensing territories—notably the U.K.—have seen corporate-licensing activity not only grow but diversify, while others have seen brand-extension licensing begin to emerge over the past few years.

The U.K. has experienced particular strength when it comes to food and beverage brands extending into the supermarket. Food trademarks such as Tango, Chewits, Guinness, Tetley, Cadbury, Haribo, Marmite, Magnum, and Hovis and restaurant chains including Pizza Express, Nando's, Wagamama, Wahaca, Gourmet Burger Kitchen, Hummingbird Bakery, La Tasca, Maison Blanc, and Carluccio's are among those moving into the grocery aisles. Automotive brands represent another substantial sector.

But corporate licensing in the U.K. has expanded well beyond these areas. Both homegrown brands, such as sporting goods label Karrimor, children's HBA brand Matey, and mattress brand Silentnight, and global brands, such as Energizer, are experiencing significant brand-extension activity.

Meanwhile, almost all other regions—particularly those that are more mature as licensing territories—are seeing a progressively higher level of brand-extension activity. Each has its unique areas of focus:

- In Brazil, sporting goods and sports lifestyle brands have established strong licensing programs, some with dozens of licensees and hundreds of products on the market. Examples include Naja Extreme, Mormaii, Red Nose, and one of the largest and longest-established programs, FICO.

- In France, magazine brands such as ELLE and Marie Claire established licensing programs long ago and are still going strong, while global brands such as Cosmopolitan have forged new deals in recent years.

- In Argentina, trendy fashion labels and fashion retail chains, often aimed at teens and young adults, have launched licensing initiatives for products such as accessories and cosmetics. Some include Kevingston, 47 Street, Muaa, John Cook, and Como Quieras Que Te Quiera.

- In Korea and China, local brands are slowly starting to dip their toes into licensing. The former has many well-established and recognized homegrown brands, but until recently they had not been involved much in brand-extension licensing. In the latter, homegrown brands had traditionally been perceived by locals as being of less quality than foreign brands, but that is starting to change and a few corporate properties, such as in electronics and fashion/retail, are looking at the potential for licensing.

Some of the properties mentioned here have their roots in non-corporate sectors (e.g. fashion or publishing), but they are using the techniques of brand-extension licensing to expand their product assortment and distribution.

Pockets of Strength

As noted, the corporate licensing sector in the U.S. and Canada has become crowded and competitive, and its growth has slowed to a degree. That said, certain niches remain vibrant:

- Technology brands such as Kodak, Nokia, Sharp, and Roku are licensing their names into a variety of electronics categories, including, in some cases, core products.

- Magazines and media brands (e.g., BeFit, Allrecipes, BabyTV) are lending their names to categories with a close fit to their content, through traditional licensing deals as well as capsules, co-branding, curation, and experiential licensing (services, restaurants). Magazines have been particularly active, especially lifestyle titles (e.g. *InStyle, GQ*) and food publications (*Bon Appetit, Cooking Light*), among others.

- Infant development brands such as Britax, Playtex, Sassy, Safety 1st, Sophie la Girafe, and Little Giraffe have extended their brands into relevant categories, including toys, books, layette, safety, and others.

- Food and beverage brands with roots in everything from fresh produce (Chiquita, Vidalia Onion, Welch's) to baking (Krusteaz) continue to expand their footprints into other supermarket aisles.

- Restaurant brand licensing is still going strong after years of fast growth, despite an increasingly crowded market. Chains from Johnny Rockets and Jamba Juice to Red Robin and Rosa Mexicano, to Sweetie Pie's and Serendipity 3 are all expanding their brands, mostly

Polaroid: Post-Bankruptcy Revival

Polaroid was one of the first brands to go into bankruptcy, then experience ownership changes, then re-establish itself through a strategy mostly based on licensing deals. Many other brands have followed suit since then.

The property's current owner, PLR Holdings, has authorized a variety of licensees to created branded products, mostly in the electronics category. They include C&A Licensing and Sakar for cameras—formerly the core of Polaroid's business—Empire Electronics for LCD TVs, and Southern Telecom for tablets, among others.

into retail foods and beverages but also occasional non-foods products.

The reasons for their respective growth trajectories vary. Some are facing strong challenges in their core industries, leading them to look to licensing for incremental revenue and/or an alternative business model. Others operate in sectors where licensing has been scarce, allowing forward-thinking licensees and/or licensors to fill the white space with licensed brand-extensions that make sense.

Aside from brand extension, corporate brands have been involved in design-driven fashion collaborations. Many of these have been food and beverage brands (Coca-Cola, Pepsi, Mountain Dew, Budweiser) that want to reach a young, trendy, upscale consumer. Others range from magazines (Playboy) to car brands (Mustang), which often use this technique to mark significant anniversaries.

Rising from the Dead

A number of corporate brands have seen their owners enter bankruptcy and liquidate. They sometimes end up being sold, often to a growing breed of investment companies that take financial stakes in dormant (and underperforming) brands with the intent to rejuvenate them, either to maintain a long-term business or to sell them off after the turnaround. Their repositioning strategies tend to focus heavily on licensing.

Some of the areas where this has taken place frequently include camera and electronics brands, with Polaroid being a leading example, and retail and restaurant brands, including Wild Oats and Tavern On the Green.

This trend is not exclusively tied to the realm of corporate licensing; defunct and struggling fashion labels, celebrity estate properties, and even classic character/entertainment brands have also experienced similar transitions. The trend is likely to continue as corporations streamline their operations and discontinue or jettison underperforming brands that still may have value with the right owner and the right strategy.

Power of Brands at Retail

Branding has become increasingly important in the eyes of consumers in recent years.

First, branded goods are gaining shelf space at the expense of private labels, marking a reversal from the trends of the recent past. Private label continues to be important in some retail channels, of course, such as in supermarkets around the world. But in many channels and in many countries, retailers and consumers are looking for recognized brands, which they believe represent quality and value.

This viewpoint extends not only to true corporate brands as defined in the licensing business, but to fashion labels and even some sports, art, or entertainment/character properties, depending on their positioning.

In addition, the consumer desirability associated with brands has given rise to co-branding deals pairing strong consumer products brands with properties from other realms. This phenomenon has long been in evidence in the food and beverage category, where the licensor's brand or property brings excitement, freshness, or flavor, while the licensee's brand brings equally important attributes such as trust, quality, and safety.

In sports licensing, it is increasingly common to pair imagery tied to a U.S. major league, global sports event, or soccer club with a key sports apparel brand, such as Nike, Adidas, or Puma. Fans want to wear the garment to show their support for their team or favorite player, but they also want the quality and performance they believe the brand provides.

As noted earlier, corporate brand-extension techniques apply to nearly any type of property. At the same time, many licensable IPs are referred to as "brands," whether or not they use these techniques.

The use of the term *brand* extends to properties that are positioned as "lifestyle properties" (another label that has become ubiquitous and has many meanings, depending on the user). So-called lifestyle properties use brand-extension tactics to enter new categories with products that reflect the "lifestyle" associated with a celebrity, an artist's imagery, a designer label's sensibility, and so on.

14 No More Middle

Developments over the last several years have creat-ed steep challenges for licensors that are positioned in "the middle." These include property owners whose price points are neither in the high-end/luxury nor discount range; that target mid-tier retail rather than specialty and department stores or mass-and-below retail tiers; that are neither global powerhouses nor focused primarily on their local market; and that are neither a giant Hollywood studio or other major licensor, nor a niche player.

A Moribund Mid-Tier

The years-long struggles of mid-tier retailers, especially in the U.S., have been well documented. As Exhibit 20 shows, the fates of the major U.S. mid-tier retail chains have varied, but all have faced and/or are continuing to face steep challenges.

Consumers are looking for either low prices or for the quality, distinctiveness, and service associated with the higher-end tiers (or sometimes both), depending on their income, circumstances, and desires. The mid-tier, which offers prices higher than mass and a level of service and quality less than department, specialty, and luxury stores, does not meet either objective.

Exhibit 20

Struggles of Selected Mid-Tier Retailers in the U.S.

Retailer	Status	Selected Licensing Activity
Mervyn's	Declared bankruptcy in mid-2008 and closed its remaining 175 locations after the 2008 holiday season. Had been privately held since its sale by Dayton-Hudson Corporation in 2004.	Had exclusive and non-exclusive relationships with a variety of licensors, ranging from classic character Miffy and fashion label Sideout to artist Ken Done.
JCPenney	Is closing 40 stores (4% of total) in 2015 after several management and strategy changes over the previous two years. Had trimmed a number of brands in 2013 and brought back others.	Has had a number of exclusive licensed lines including the controversial Martha Stewart deal, Michael Graves, Joe Fresh, Jonathan Adler, Terrence Conrad, Liz Claiborne (later purchased outright), and many more.
Sears	Has experienced a long run of financial losses and continues to look for ways to cut costs, including through layoffs and store closures. Has announced it would close 200+ stores across Sears and Kmart in 2015.	Recent exclusives range from Matthew McConaughey and Seventeen to The Kardashians, NBA, and Outdoor Life. Has had abundant involvement in licensing over the years.

Source: Raugust Communications

This movement away from the middle does not just affect the major mid-tier chains in the exhibit, but any specialty store or regional department store that targets the middle.

Deals with mid-tier chains such as JCPenney and Sears have not gone away, of course; Jones Group licensed its Black Label by Evan Picone brand to the former, while the latter launched an exclusive Seventeen clothing line, supplied by licensee Adjmi Apparel Group, both in 2014. But the focus tends to be on either the high or low end (or both, depending on the property), rather than the middle in most cases.

That said, the lines are blurring, especially as the luxury market is starting to see its fortunes waver in 2014 and early 2015 after several years of strength. Some developments that illustrate this phenomenon:

- More luxury designers such as Balmain have launched "affordable luxury" or diffusion labels. These products are still priced at the high end of the market but not in the top luxury tier for which these couturiers are known.

- The longstanding fast fashion trend continues to bring luxury designers such as Alexander Wang, Karl Lagerfeld, Jean Paul Gaultier, and Stella McCartney into lower-priced retail chains such as H&M, Uniqlo, Target, and Lindex.

- Mass and luxury are merging through capsule collections in which a high-end designer interprets film imagery or classic characters.

Limited programs in the last classification—think SpongeBob with London-based luxury designer Beatrix Ong—generate publicity and can spur sales for both the designer's luxury business and the entertainment property's mass products.

Global Powerhouses Versus Niche Players

On a worldwide basis, the properties that do best tend to be those that are globally renowned and owned by the largest licensors. These major players have the clout to secure shelf space not only for their classic properties, but for their newer introductions as well. Disney and several of the other major Hollywood studios are examples, as are well-known fashion labels from Ralph Lauren to Cherokee, corporate brands from Pepsi-Cola to Philips, and celebrities from Jamie Oliver to Paris Hilton.

Although there are exceptions (see: Angry Birds), these are the properties that tend to collectively account for a large percentage of shelf space and of retail sales of licensed goods around the world. This is true in established territories such as in Western Europe or Australia; growing regions such as Latin America, Central and Eastern Europe, or the Middle East; and even emerging territories where licensing is just starting to take hold.

On the other hand, the global licensors' greatest competition in each market consists of homegrown IP, both classic and new. These local properties may be relatively unknown outside their homeland, but rival the Cartoon Networks and Coca-Colas of the world within their own boundaries. Examples, depending on the territory, may include local TV characters; football/soccer, cricket, and rugby athletes and teams; fashion designers and artists; local celebrities from entertainment and other walks of life; and, increasingly, corporate brands. Some can generate sales of licensed merchandise equal to or more than the global powers on a local basis.

Some of these homegrown properties are starting to cross borders, mostly to neighboring countries but increasingly with designs on markets all over the world.

The "no-more-middle" phenomenon also applies to the size and scope of the audience a licensor and its licensees want to reach. Some properties are reaching for as wide a fan base as possible, across multiple distribution channels. Others are narrowly targeted toward a niche but avid consumer group through a small number of distribution points that cater to those fans. Both can be successful when measured against their respective objectives.

Of course, many properties are neither global brands nor local powerhouses, neither mass nor niche, neither luxury nor low-end. These are the ones that face the steepest competitive barriers when it comes to securing licensees and distribution, as well as attracting the attention of consumers.

Licensing executives used to comment that not all properties could be home runs, but that a double or a triple could still represent a nice business. Today, however, it seems that home runs and singles are the results for most plate appearances. Doubles and triples are increasingly difficult to achieve.

15 Evolution, Not Revolution

Occasionally, brand new properties or property types will break through and hit it big. Or brand-new products will come on the scene and create possibilities for the licensing community that did not exist before.

While these opportunities are real, most of the advances in licensing these days are more about evolution than revolution. Innovation tends to focus on adding a twist or moving toward the fringes of existing categories, property types, retail channels, or geographic regions, rather than conquering new frontiers.

Mining The Archives

On the property side, this type of evolution shows itself in a variety of ways. In the entertainment sector, for example, licensors are increasingly creating programs that involve secondary characters. The Disney Villains program, for example, was a way for the studio to add new opportunities for licensees beyond the Disney Princess and other leading franchises, as well as a way to test for potentially break-out characters.

Other licensors are looking for ways to incorporate behind-the-scenes personnel or guest stars to generate excitement among their best fans. For the Simpsons, licensor Fox and its collectibles licensee NECA added 25 new figures, from Kid Rock to Hugh Hefner, to their action figure line. Each was a replica of the Simpsonized version of the star from his or her TV guest spot.

Producers, directors, and creators such as George Lucas (Star Wars), Peter Jackson (Lord of the Rings), and Stan Lee (Spiderman) have appeared as characters in licensed products based on those properties, from action figures to comic books. In sports licensing, Major League Baseball licensee Topps launched a First Pitch series of trading cards in 2015, commemorating celebrities who have thrown out the ceremonial first pitch before MLB games.

It should be noted that these ventures extend opportunities for existing fans to purchase more products and for existing licensees to expand their product assortment. They are less likely to bring in brand new fans or new licensees.

New Technologies, New Opportunities

The digital realm provides an interesting example of this theory of evolution, because it has gone through the process so quickly. Before 2010, the idea of any property from the digital world being positioned as licensable was still novel. Then came Angry Birds, the mobile game that launched in 2009 and started introducing merchandise in 2010-2011. It quickly became a global success story in almost every territory around the world.

That led to a burst of mobile properties becoming available for licensing, from Fruit Ninja and Cut the Rope to Temple Doom and many more. Many licensors within that group continue to sign licensees and offer merchandise to consumers as of 2015, but none to date have achieved the status of "the next Angry Birds."

At about the same time, virtual worlds such as Club Penguin and Moshi Monsters were attracting significant groups of members and fans, and a number of licensing programs debuted. Some of these have been successful in certain territories (e.g. Moshi Monsters in the U.K.), but the sector as a whole never reached the levels of merchandise sales that were once expected.

The early focus on mobile apps and virtual worlds quickly moved into other areas of the digital world, starting with bloggers (covering food, family issues, design/style, and other topics) and YouTube celebrities, then to properties emanating from other social media platforms (Twitter, Instagram, Pinterest, Vine).

Most of the programs to date are more niche than mass, aiming squarely for the properties' digital followers (who often number in the millions) with products closely related to the content and mostly achieved through short-term collaborations. A number of these efforts are succeeding, based on expectations in these early days. And new celebrities and brands are being born through social media channels every week. As a result, the digital-origin sector is likely to continue expanding quickly for the foreseeable future, moving from platform to platform as new channels of distribution develop.

Looking Beyond The Top Properties

Another example of this evolutionary outlook is in the collegiate sector. Historically, the top revenue-generating universities attracted most of the attention in terms of licensing, especially those with a lot of championships in key televised sports such as football and basketball.

In recent years, however, mid-sized universities have been increasing their focus on licensing as a means of generating revenue. These opportunities also are becoming more attractive to licensees and the major collegiate licensing agencies, both of which are looking for ways to expand their businesses.

A handful of the universities placing more emphasis on licensing, and seeing their licensing revenues rise in the past few years, include the likes of Marshall University, North Dakota State, University of Tennessee-Chattanooga, Miami-Ohio, and Ball State, among many others.

The spark that causes these institutions to invest more resources into expanding licensing is often an improvement in their sports performance, such as winning a championship within their NCAA division. Excellence in sports is a key driver of merchandise sales for these mid-sized schools, as it is for the larger universities.

But other factors also play a role, including improved e-commerce and retail distribution, retention of a licensing agency, improved marketing and promotion, an expanded product mix, or a redesigned logo.

Products on the Fringe

The evolution of new product categories is following a similar trajectory as the evolution of property types. Brand new categories spring up from time to time, of course, often tech-related (e.g., fitness bands or mobile-payment devices). But much of licensing executives' focus is on seeking new opportunities that are adjacent to established categories.

Alcohol, which used to be taboo for most properties, is one example. Several years ago, licensors including chefs, golfers, musicians, entertainment studios, fashion designers, artists, and more began licensing or otherwise extending their names into the wine category.

Once that sector became crowded, property owners began to move into beer, then into other liquor categories. Vodkas have attracted a large number of deals, while limoncello, bourbon, tequila, and more have seen some licensing activity. Some pairings involve flavor profiles (e.g., MoonPie whiskey and Cinnabon vodka), but most are more traditional brand-extension or celebrity deals. Licensing continues to extend into new areas of the alcohol industry; in 2014, for example, came a licensed sake (with chef Akira Back).

The pet products industry has taken a similar path. A bustling sector for licensing for more than five years, it has become crowded with properties across property types (from singer Bret Michaels to apparel brand Dickies). For the most part, these deals have encompassed the whole range of pet products (usually excluding food), although a few (e.g. Arm & Hammer) have brought functional benefits to the category.

In 2014, more agreements began to emerge that focused on pockets of the industry that either had not yet been targeted specifically or matched the specific functional or other attributes of the brand being licensed (or both). Examples included ecologically sound waste disposal from Animal Planet and Greenberry; products for pets outside of the usual cats and dogs (e.g. reptiles, gerbils, birds, and fish) from National Geographic and PetSmart; neoprene apparel, flotation devices, and other items from Body Glove and Plangea; and pet toys from Wham-O (owner of Frisbee, Superball, and Hula Hoop) and Precious Tales.

Even in the apparel category, where it seems licensors have mined all options, there are incremental growth opportunities. In 2014, larger sizes for women, which often have been left out of licensing deals, became an area of focus, with a number of celebrities and designers, from Isabel Toledo to Kelly Osbourne, launching programs that either focus on larger sizes or include those as part of a whole spectrum of sizing. Previously, the formerly-untapped maternity segment was a key area of interest.

New Retail Niches

The retail channels and individual retailers that historically have been the strongest supporters of licensing have become more and more saturated with licensed products. Consequently, they have become increasingly selective about which properties and products they will carry. Marketers of licensed products are thus looking in new directions for opportunities, not just in terms of e-commerce and other digital channels but on the bricks-and-mortar front as well.

At the same time, retail chains that have not traditionally been involved with licensed merchandise are recognizing the benefit of licensing to add some consumer buzz and offer something exclusive to their shoppers. This is particularly true as many chains continue to struggle and seek new business models or strategies to give them an edge.

As noted in Chapter 11, examples of retail channels that have recently expanded their licensing activities (especially with DTR and exclusive deals) have ranged from electronics chains such as Best Buy, which has forged agreements with Kate Spade, Isaac Mizrahi, and other designers to give it an advantage in electronics accessories, to fashion retailers such as Dress Barn and its sister chain Lane Bryant, both of which have entered into licensing deals for the first time.

Geographic Frontiers

The major, mature territories for licensing are teeming with properties and products fighting for attention. Meanwhile, even emerging territories such as the BRIC countries have become significantly more competitive than just a few years ago. They also are starting to see a slowdown in the fast pace of growth they have experienced in the past several years, due to changes in their economies and the maturation of their local licensing businesses.

Exhibit 21

The Next Frontier: Emerging Geographic Territories for Licensing?

Region of Interest	Selected Countries in Region	Adjacent Major Territory or Territories
Commonweath of Independent States (CIS), Baltic states, and other nearby countries	Ukraine, Uzbekistan, Belarus, Georgia, Latvia, Estonia, Kazakhstan, Lithuania, Slovenia	Russia
South Asian Association for Regional Cooperation (SAARC)	Bangladesh, Pakistan, Sri Lanka, Bhutan, Afghanistan	India
Central America/ Caribbean	Nicaragua, Honduras, Guatemala, Panama, Dominican Republic	Mexico, northern South America
Sub-Saharan Africa	Angola, Kenya, Mozambique, Namibia, Nigeria, Tanzania, Zimbabwe	Middle East/North Africa (MENA), South Africa

Source: Raugust Communications

As the landscapes in established territories become more difficult, global licensors seeking increases in revenues are looking to truly untapped regions for potential. Although there have been sporadic deals in many of these countries for years, they face steep economic, cultural, social, political, and other challenges. When there were more and easier-to-seize opportunities elsewhere, they were not a priority, to say the least.

Expanding Geographic Boundaries

Licensors increasingly are taking advantage of opportunities that present themselves in undeveloped licensing territories, particularly as part of deals that center on more established countries nearby.

Williamson-Dickie, for example, signed ID Overseas Private Limited to design, manufacture, market, and sell licensed products in India, in a 10-year deal that included a variety of apparel and footwear categories. In addition, the agreement authorized ID Overseas to distribute in Pakistan, Nepal, Bangladesh, and Sri Lanka, none of which are key territories for licensing.

While not necessarily a strategic imperative, such expansion often makes sense opportunistically as a way to test the viability of new territories and generate incremental sales with relatively low risk.

That scenario has started to change, however. A few licensors are beginning to consider some of these brand-new territories as ripe for exploration, at least as an ancillary business that can piggyback on more established regions nearby. Exhibit 21 shows some key areas of interest.

The beginnings of a small local licensing business are also becoming evident in several of these countries. In Bangladesh, for example, 2014 brought a licensing program tied to a global 26-team cricket competition that was held in Dhaka, with merchandise including apparel, bags, caps, and collectibles sold at the venue and at several retail chains, from Texmart to Intersport. Bangladesh also has been on global licensors' radar as well, often as an add-on to their Indian deals.

Most of these countries remain extremely problematic in terms of licensing, and revenues and attention will in all likelihood remain ancillary for some time. But the combination of global licensors dipping their toes into these markets and the slow development of homegrown licensing initiatives should help further the potential. It is too soon to say how quickly that will occur, however, or which territories will emerge first.

Conclusion

Some of the specific trends discussed in this report, such as 3D printing and wearable technology, came on the scene quickly in 2014 after being barely on the radar the previous year. Others, such as user-generated content and licensed properties with roots in social media, transitioned from virtual novelties to diverse, commonplace, and/or long-term trends. Still others, such as celebrity licensing, are ongoing but became more deeply entrenched in 2014.

Individual trends such as these come and go increasingly quickly. But they also are components of the broader, longer-term trends that are here to stay. The latter—the 15 licensing super trends discussed in this report—can serve as a blueprint for licensing executives as they create their strategic plans for the next three or more years.

The interrelated nature of these overriding trends is illustrated by the fact that many individual licensing initiatives reflect several of the 15, as well as incorporating multiple specific trends within each:

- Jillian Michaels' deal with Kmart for a line of Impact by Jillian Michaels performance activewear illustrates the continued strength of celebrity, the health and wellness trend, the inclusion of functional and performance attributes into licensed merchandise, and the ongoing quest for retail exclusives.

- Target's limited-edition girls' collection tied to the film *Annie*, created in collaboration with costume designer Renee Ehrlich Kalfus, reflects the increasing diversity of the celebrity sector, the prominence of limited editions and capsule collections, and the importance of fan engagement (a DIY fashion design kit was included as one of the 25 items).

- PBS Kids' deal to distribute toys through Whole Foods highlights the connection between licensing and promotion, the role of "doing good" (natural and organic products, charity tie-ins, educational elements), and the hunt for alternative distribution channels.

- Korean designer JuunJ's network of global pop-up shops illustrates the importance of experiential ventures across property types, the expansion of local properties from a variety of territories on a global scale, and the role of artists in a diverse range of licensing initiatives (Josh Luke was a collaborator).

Not only are there interrelationships between the 15 super trends discussed in this report, and the shorter-term trends they encompass, but there are several broader themes that run through and help drive almost all of them:

- The ever-faster pace of change, which requires continual innovation and also makes it difficult to repeat successful initiatives.

- The need to guard against risk.

- The quest for flexibility in deal structures, in the hopes of allocating investments and rewards more equitably.

- The continuing search for avenues of incremental growth as traditional licensing segments become saturated.

RaugustReports Presents: 15 Licensing Super Trends for 2015 and Beyond represents a snapshot of the licensing business as it stands in early 2015. Many of the individual trends will go away quickly, replaced by new developments, many unforeseen. Some of the trends that are just emerging at the beginning of 2015 will never become established.

That said, the overriding "super trends" discussed here will continue to provide a blueprint for all kinds of innovation in licensing that will arise over the next several years, no matter what specific form it may take.

About the Author

Karen Raugust is the founder of Raugust Communications, publisher of *Raugust Reports: A Blog About Licensing* and other licensing information. She has been covering and consulting on the licensing business since 1990, when she joined *The Licensing Letter* as Executive Editor, serving in that position for six years. More recently, she was the long-time Special Projects Editor for *TLL*. In that role, she contributed articles to the newsletter and wrote books and research reports including *The Licensing Business Handbook, International Licensing: A Status Report, The Licensing Letter Food and Beverage Report*, and many more.

Karen also is the Licensing Correspondent and a Contributing Editor for *Publishers Weekly*, where she writes a column, news, and features about licensed book publishing. She has covered licensing for other publications as well, including *Animation Magazine, Animation World Network, American Artist, Billboard, Street & Smith's Sports Business Journal, U.S. Art,* and *Variety Jr.* Other clients for her writing and editing services include Simba Information, Meritas, and *Blueprints Quarterly Journal*.

About Raugust Communications

Raugust Communications provides accurate, timely information and data about the trends and issues facing global property owners, manufacturers, retailers, and others involved in the business of licensing. Karen Raugust, who has covered the licensing business since 1990, authors the publications, which focus on how-to topics, market research, and trend information.

The company's mission is to fill gaps in the market for licensing information by addressing topics not adequately covered by other resources; provide information that is accessible to everyone in licensing, from beginner to expert and from the smallest entrepreneur to the biggest corporation; offer context and meaning by finding the connections between all of the individual news announcements appearing in licensing executives' in-boxes every day; and identify the trends that will affect, disrupt, and transform the licensing business in the months and years ahead.

Raugust Communications' publications include *RaugustReports: A Blog On Licensing* and *RaugustReports Presents: 15 Licensing Super Trends for 2015 and Beyond.* Visit www.raugustcommunications.com/licensing for more information.

www.ingramcontent.com/pod-product-compliance
Lightning Source LLC
Chambersburg PA
CBHW071940220326
41599CB00033BA/6557

9 781942 917007